Bulldogs

TAMMY GAGNE

Bulldogs

Project Team
Editor: Heather Russell-Revesz
Copy Editor: Ellen Bingham
Interior Design: Leah Lococo Ltd. and Stephanie Krautheim
Design Layout: Patricia Escabi

T.F.H. Publications
President/CEO: Glen S. Axelrod
Executive Vice President: Mark E. Johnson
Publisher: Christopher T. Reggio
Production Manager: Kathy Bontz

T.F.H. Publications, Inc.
One TFH Plaza
Third and Union Avenues
Neptune City, NJ 07753

Discovery Communications, Inc. Book Development Team
Marjorie Kaplan, President, Animal Planet Media
Carol LeBlanc, Vice President, Licensing
Elizabeth Bakacs, Vice President, Creative Services
Brigid Ferraro, Director, Licensing
Peggy Ang, Director, Animal Planet Marketing
Caitlin Erb, Licensing Specialist

Printed and bound in China
07 08 09 10 11 1 3 5 7 9 8 6 4 2

Library of Congress Cataloging-in-Publication Data
Gagne, Tammy
Bulldogs / Tammy Gagne.
p. cm. — (Animal planet pet care library)
Includes index.
ISBN 978-0-7938-3783-0 (alk. paper) 1. Bulldogs. I. Title.
SF429.J27M67 2007
636.755—dc22
2007005847

This book has been published with the intent to provide accurate and authoritative information in regard to the subject matter within. While every reasonable precaution has been taken in preparation of this book, the author and publisher expressly disclaim responsibility for any errors, omissions, or adverse effects arising from the use or application of the information contained herein. The techniques and suggestions are used at the reader's discretion and are not to be considered a substitute for veterinary care. If you suspect a medical problem consult your veterinarian.

The Leader In Responsible Animal Care For Over 50 Years!™
www.tfh.com

CENTRAL
Garden & Pet

Table of Contents

Chapter 1

Why I Adore My

Bulldog

"Everything that is right about the Bulldog is wrong on most other dogs—and vice versa," says American Kennel Club Non-Sporting Group judge Keke Kahn. One simply doesn't hear terms such as *thickset* and *short-faced* used so often and with such positive connotation as with this charmingly distinctive breed. It is not merely the Bulldog's physical characteristics that make this breed a unique one, though. The dog's personality plays an equally important role in his massive appeal. He is kind, steadfast, and loyal—everything an owner could want in a canine companion.

Fortunately, A Thing of the Past

The word *Bulldog* was first used at the end of the 16th century, when bullbaiting contests were prevalent. This horrific sport, which was enormously popular during Europe's Middle Ages, centered on the dog's pinning and holding of a bull's nose, a highly sensitive area. This effectively rendered the bull virtually helpless. Although the dogs were trained to remain low in an effort to thwart the bull's defensive use of its horns, a great many dogs were killed nonetheless as a result of being thrown into the air—or from being gored afterward if they miraculously survived the landing.

The pastime's popularity created a strong demand for dogs capable of competing in these grueling events. The Mastiff-like ancestors to our present-day Bulldogs were originally larger and heavier than the breed we know today. This shortcoming, as it was then seen, was addressed by altering the size and stature through a more deliberate breeding process. Through outcrosses, for example, the bulk of the dog's weight was shifted toward the head, making it more difficult for a bull to break a dog's back when shaking him. Not surprisingly, these early breeders possessed a rather single-minded approach to temperament: the more vicious and tenacious, the better, they thought.

Although England's House of Commons rejected a bill to ban

A High Price to Pay

Although bullbaiting was widely know as a spectator sport for royalty and noblemen, many historians assert that there was a more practical purpose for this dreadful pastime. It was widely believed that the baiting of a bull made its flesh more tender and nutritious. In fact, a butcher who sold the meat of a bull that had not been baited prior to slaughtering would be held accountable for this significant transgression, and the meat would be rendered unfit for human consumption.

bullbaiting in 1802, an act of parliament finally made it illegal in 1835. Sadly, though, the activity continued underground for many years after this time. As this sadistic sport slowly died out, the demand for Bulldogs also waned. Fortunately, a small group of faithful fanciers managed to keep the breed from becoming extinct.

Keeping the Breed Alive

In 1864, a group of about 30 Bulldog enthusiasts joined together to form the first unofficial Bulldog club. This initial club, headed by a man named R. S.

Rockstro, lasted only three years. In this short period, though, the group nonetheless managed to pen the first Bulldog breed standard, known as the Philo Kuan.

The enduring Bulldog Club of the United Kingdom was subsequently formed in London in 1875, even before the development of England's Kennel Club (KC). A second standard was drawn up at that time, though it varied only slightly from the Philo Kuan. One of the specifications limited the size a Bulldog could be, for at this time Spanish Bulldogs were weighing in at 100 pounds or more. The Bulldog Club and the London Bulldog Society (another famous organization) both favored a more conservatively sized dog.

America's official recognition of the Bulldog began in New England, when H. D. Kendall of Lowell, Massachusetts, established the Bulldog Club of America (BCA) in 1890, the same year the breed was granted official recognition by the American Kennel Club (AKC). By the 1950s, the BCA was a national organization in every sense of the word, with geographical divisions a direct result of its growth.

Membership in one of these regional branches constituted membership in the BCA. The club began by using the UK's standard but decided to create a more descriptive standard of its own in 1896.

English, American, or French?

Although some owners proudly refer to their dogs as *English* Bulldogs, neither the AKC nor the KC uses the word *English* (or *American*) in this breed's official name. No matter which side of the Atlantic your breeder calls home, never let anyone convince you that geography plays a part in producing a quality Bulldog. All Bulldogs have the same English heritage, and there are both principled and unprincipled breeders everywhere. What matters most is the careful selection of a dog's more recent lineage.

A French Bulldog, on the other hand, *is* a separate breed. This dog, along with several other breeds—including the

Despite his checkered past, the Bulldog is a fun-loving companion.

Bullmastiff, the Bull Terrier, and the Boston Terrier—was produced by crossing the Bulldog into its lines at one point or another.

Physical Characteristics

The Bulldog has a distinctive look all his own.

Size

Today the size for an adult male Bulldog is approximately 50 pounds (23 kg), and for a female, 40 pounds (18 kg). Weight isn't the only area in which female dogs are held to a slightly different standard. According to the AKC, females are generally given a little extra latitude in the areas of size, proportion, and symmetry, as they are not thought to match the breed's standard as closely as do the male dogs. (Many owners of champion females disagree with this position, though!)

Eyes

The Bulldog's eyes should be situated low on the skull, as far from the ears and as wide apart from each other

A True Southern Gentleman

For decades, Bulldogs have been the mascots of such eminent organizations as the United States Marines and Yale University. They have also been owned by some famous people. Just a few examples of this diverse group are George Clooney, Iced T, Vincent Price, and Truman Capote. One of the best-known Bulldogs, though, is Uga, the legendary mascot of the University of Georgia. For more than 50 years, this celebrated member of the team has always been the solid white son of the previous mascot. The biggest of them all, Uga VI (known more formally as Uga V's Whatchagot Loran) weighs 63 pounds (29 kg) and was born in 1999. With several impressive seasons under his belt, Uga VI has done an excellent job of representing his team. He has been named the Best College Mascot by both Turner South Broadcasting and Southern Sports Awards. Still, he has yet to surpass the fame of his father, Uga V (Uga IV's Magillicuddy II), whose list of credits includes a *Sports Illustrated* cover and an appearance in the provocative film *Midnight in the Garden of Good and Evil*. Both Uga and his owner, Frank "Sonny" Seiler, make appearances in this movie, which was filmed in their hometown of Savannah. Don't even think of asking how you can get an Uga puppy of your own, though. Proud as he may be of this impressive line that his family has owned for more than half a century, Seiler will not under any circumstances sell puppies to the public or provide stud services to breeders. If you want to experience the distinctive Uga spirit, you'll just have to attend a game.

as possible. The outer corners should not venture beyond the outline of the cheeks when viewed from the front. The specifications for a dog's eyes are many: round, moderately sized, neither sunken nor bulging, and very dark in color. The lids should cover the whites of the eyes when the dog is looking forward, and the inner membrane should never be seen.

Ears

In contrast to the eyes, the ears should sit high on the dog's head. A so-called rose-eared shape is ideal. This means that the ear folds inward at its back lower edge while the upper front edge curls over, outward, and backward—exposing the burr, the visible part of the ear's interior. Ears should not be carried upright (as in prick-eared breeds), and they must never be cropped.

Head

A Bulldog's head should be quite large, and when viewed from the side, it should appear very high and short from the dog's nose to the back of his head. The forehead should be flat, never rounded or domed. It should be neither overly prominent nor hanging over the dog's face. Well-rounded cheeks should protrude

outward beyond the eyes. This, combined with the short muzzle, affords the breed its unique expression. The nostrils should be wide, large, and black. A nose of any color other than black is considered objectionable, but a brown or liver-colored nose is grounds for outright disqualification. The teeth should be large and strong but only barely visible when the dog's mouth is closed.

Body

Like the Bulldog's head, the neck should be short. Deep and strong, it should arch at the beginning of the back. The body should have full sides and well-rounded ribs. The overall appearance should be broad and low but without a rotund belly. A Bulldog is rugged, not overweight.

The Bulldog's wrinkles are one of his distinguishing features.

The Bulldog has muscular shoulders that slant outward.

feet should be of moderate size. The front feet may turn outward slightly, or they may be straight. The hind feet, however, should always point outward.

Coat

A Bulldog's coat, like nearly everything else about this breed, is short, but it should also be straight and flat.

SENIOR DOG TIP
A Dog's Life

Dogs are considered senior citizens when they move into the final third of their lives. For Bulldogs, this is typically between the ages of 6 and 7 years. With the ever-advancing technology of modern medicine and the benefits of sound nutrition, though, some Bulldogs are living to be as old as 12, postponing those golden years even further.

  The best way to ensure that your Bulldog will live a long and healthy life is to use balance and moderation. Feed your dog healthy food but not too much of it. Make sure he gets enough exercise, but don't overdo it. And try not to stress over every little problem that brings you to the vet's office, but always keep that appointment!

Tail

The tail may be straight or spiraled but should never be curved or curly. It is short and should hang low and close to the body. With a thick base, the tail should narrow toward the tip. No portion of a so-called screwed tail should ever be elevated above the base (or root).

Shoulders and Legs

A Bulldog's muscular shoulders should slant outward, indicating stability and power. The legs should be short, stout, and set wide apart. The hind legs should be a bit longer than the front, and the

Additionally, it should be smooth, glossy, and of fine texture. The skin should be soft and loose—particularly at the head, neck, and shoulders. Heavy wrinkling on the head and face is desirable. There should be two loose pendulous folds located between the jaw and the chest; this is called the dewlap.

Colors

Interestingly, all colors are not considered equal. Listed in order of preference, the acceptable colors are:

- Red brindle
- All other brindles
- Solid white
- Solid red, fawn, or fallow
- Piebald (spotted or patched)

Color should be uniform, pure, and brilliant. Quality always takes precedence. For instance, a fine-looking piebald is preferable to an inferior brindle or solid. Black patches may be acceptable (as long as, like other colored patches, they are evenly distributed), but a solid black color is considered highly undesirable. In brindles and solid colors, a small white patch on a dog's chest will not hamper him in the ring.

Movement

When a Bulldog is shown, it is truly an unusual display. Unlike other breeds, whose gaits are described as balanced, smooth, and effortless, the Bulldog

The Expert Knows

Swimming

Most of us are familiar with the old wives' tale that assures us all dogs can swim. The Bulldog proves to be an exception to this well-known, albeit erroneous, assumption. Owners must always be extra vigilant when their dogs are near water. Children's wading pools may be an excellent means of keeping a Bulldog cool on a hot day, but anything deeper than this means that a life jacket will be necessary.

moves in a loose-jointed and shuffling sideways motion. He *rolls*. This is not to say that his movements are without merit. On the contrary, the Bulldog's gait is also unrestrained, free, and vigorous—much like the dog himself.

Mr. Personality

An owner couldn't ask for a kinder companion than a Bulldog. While his physical features may seem rather unbalanced to the uninitiated, his temperament is anything but uneven. His demeanor is calming but courageous. He would go to the ends of the earth for those he loves. He wears his heart on his sleeve—or, more specifically, on his animated face, which exudes expression (a delightfully sour expression).

This is a calm but courageous breed.

parents, so be sure to ask to see a puppy's dam and sire before deciding to purchase a particular dog. The selection of breeding stock should be a painstaking process. Only dogs with the best temperaments and physical characteristics should be bred in the first place. Beware of any breeder who is unwilling to introduce you to your future puppy's parents for this reason.

Because Bulldogs are so *high maintenance*, many dogs purchased impetuously end up in rescue when their owners finally realize the degree of care this breed requires. Extensive consideration must be given to purchasing a Bulldog puppy. Adopting a dog in need of a home can be a great way to find an excellent pet, but if money is a concern, remember that Bulldogs are not only expensive at the outset; they are also a costly breed in terms of their many health issues.

Even with all their charms, though, Bulldogs are not right for everyone. The breed demands a great deal of attention. They must also be trained, for although most Bulldogs have pleasant personalities, they tend to be extremely stubborn and can easily knock people over if not taught proper manners at an early age. This exuberance and tenacity are best harnessed while a puppy is young, in order to aid in the training process instead of working against it once the dog has become more set in his ways.

Meet the Parents
Nothing is a better indicator of temperament than an individual dog's

Exercise Requirements
Of course, all dogs need exercise, but Bulldogs require less than most other dogs. At the same time, many deeply enjoy being active and make ideal family pets. Owners should draw the

How Are They With Children?

Of all the bull breeds, the Bulldog is known for being the best with children, but kids must understand the importance of being gentle. A kindergartner should be old enough to help train a Bulldog puppy, but a toddler may likely interfere with a critical element—consistency. A younger child may also be a poor match for an excited puppy, who can easily knock youngsters right off their feet by simply being his energetic self. For this reason, many breeders recommend an adult dog (at least three years old) for families with young kids. A well-trained adult dog is less likely to jump on your child, destroy toys or other belongings, or steal food from his or her hand. Older children, on the other hand, may be perfectly suited to helping raise and care for a Bulldog puppy as it grows into an equally playful yet milder-mannered adult.

line at such physically demanding activities as jogging, though, which is simply too hard on this breed's joints. If you can stand their snoring, most Bulldogs will happily follow you from room to room just to lie at your feet.

Sensitive Skin

The best time to exercise your Bulldog is early in the morning and late in the afternoon, but even at these milder times, don't forget to shield him from the sun. Bulldogs, particularly white ones, are extremely susceptible to sunburn.

One of the best places to take your Bulldog for his daily workout is your own backyard. A daily game of tag or ball—in the shade of your favorite tree, of course—can serve as the perfect physical fitness plan for this breed.

Special Needs

Bulldogs are impressively intelligent, but they do not always know what is best for them. This is why owners must be aware of their special needs. The most prominent of these is their need to be kept cool. Since this breed overheats so easily, it is imperative that owners do not leave their dogs in temperatures higher than 70°F (21°C) without ice water, and, whenever possible, air conditioning. Also, consider placing a towel under your Bulldog's water bowl, since you can expect him to slobber profusely after each and every drink.

Why I Adore My Bulldog

Chapter 2

The Stuff Of

Everyday Life

If your dog could give you a list of all the things he needs, the simplicity of it would likely surprise you. Many owners often joke that their Bulldogs would eat their way clear through a 40-pound (18 kg) bag of dog food if given the chance, but even this—deep down—is a bit of an exaggeration. Sure, dogs like to indulge in their favorite things, but even they eventually tire of the ones that, in the long run, have little impact on their well being.

Although there are numerous products and gadgets that promise to make our dogs the happiest and healthiest canines on the block, many of these items, unfortunately, do not live up to their claims. This doesn't mean that you should never splurge on superfluous toys or thingamabobs. I occasionally buy my dogs things I know they don't need, but in general, I try to pass on the things that seem doomed for disinterest from the start. (Hint: If they haven't touched it in the last month, they won't miss it if you toss it!) The things your Bulldog truly needs aren't numerous, but they should always be the first items on your shopping list.

Bed

Although many owners readily share their beds with their dogs, the decision to allow your Bulldog to sleep with you is not merely an issue of whether the dog should be allowed on the furniture. A tall bed can be a precarious place. A single jump or fall could cause a broken leg or other serious injury. If your dog must sleep in your bed, consider buying a set of canine stairs and training your

Bulldgos

The Expert Knows

Bringing Your New Dog Home

So you've taken the plunge and adopted a dog of your own. Congratulations! But what do you do now? No doubt you're excited and looking forward to forging a lifelong friendship with your new buddy. But try to keep in mind the confusion he is feeling right now. Whatever his past history, coming home with you is a new experience. He is likely to be a little disoriented, wondering where he is and who all these new people are. The key to helping your new dog make a successful adjustment to your home is being prepared and being patient. It can take anywhere from two days to two months for you and your pet to adjust to each other.

(Courtesy of the Humane Society of the United States)

dog to use them whenever getting on or off the bed.

A better place for your dog to sleep is in a bed of his own. Dog beds are available in a huge variety of fabrics and styles, but functionality should always take precedence. If the bed isn't comfortable, your dog won't use it. An older Bulldog may appreciate a bed made from orthopedic foam or the new memory foam so popular in today's mattresses. If your dog uses a crate, this is a safe spot for your Bulldog overnight. It can also serve as an efficient starter bed for a puppy that may likely ruin a conventional dog bed.

Collar

Collars made of nylon are usually the most versatile, since nylon is lightweight, easy to clean, and available in a wide selection of colors and patterns. Leather collars are also considerably durable, but most do not offer the added benefit of breakaway technology.

You can use a measuring tape to determine the size of your dog's neck. Place the tape around his neck, but make sure you are able to fit two fingers comfortably between your Bulldog's neck and the tape.

Harness

Some owners prefer to use a harness instead of a collar. Worn around the chest, a harness can help prevent a talented wriggler from escaping his owner. It is also a highly preferable choice for a Bulldog who suffers from respiratory problems. Like the collar, you can

measure your Bulldog for a harness, but instead of placing the measuring tape around the neck, it should be placed around your dog's chest, just behind his front legs.

Crate

Of all the things you will purchase for your new Bulldog, the largest will probably be his crate. Since this will also be one of the more expensive items you purchase, some time should be taken to make sure you select a model that best suits your Bulldog. I generally prefer hard plastic crates, because they offer both a safe enclosure and the added benefit of privacy, which seems to be an essential feature for my dogs. Your Bulldog may prefer the wire variety, though, especially if he has an extraverted personality.

17

A harness is a good choice for dogs with respiratory problems.

When selecting a crate, the most important consideration is size. It is vital that you choose a model that is large enough for your hefty pet. This would be an easy task if not for one other thing—it also mustn't be too big. If you buy a crate that is just a bit too large, you will lose the housetraining advantage. Your Bulldog's crate should be spacious enough for him to stand up and turn around in but not so roomy that he can decide to use one end as a makeshift bathroom.

Finally, don't forget to add something soft and comfy to the interior. A full array of crate liners is available at most pet supply stores. I strongly recommend having at least two, as they can then be rotated on laundry day.

Of course, you may opt not to provide your dog with a crate at all,

and if this is the case, rest assured you are not alone. Many smart and loving dog owners do not feel the need to use a crate. Likewise, some dogs simply don't take to this item. Particularly if your dog came from a puppy mill, he may have a deep-seated aversion to crates. In this delicate situation, it is best to respect your dog's feelings and not force him to use this elective item.

Exercise Pen (X-Pen)

A great way to offer your Bulldog the chance to safely run around off lead while outdoors is by providing him with an exercise pen, more commonly called an x-pen. This freestanding structure consists of several sides that collapse for easy use practically anywhere—even inside your home if you have the space. Some even come with

Doggie Daycare

If you worry that your Bulldog may be lonely while you're away from home each day, consider using the services of doggie daycare. This business, which works much the same way as a children's daycare center, can provide your dog with all the attention and stimulation you fear he is missing during the week while you work. Just as you carefully select someone to care for your children in your absence, you must use good judgment here, as well. When interviewing a potential provider, request a tour of the facilities and ask any questions you may have before committing to a program. Among the most important pieces of information are the number of caregivers (the ratio should be at least one provider for every 10 dogs) and the prerequisites for admission (vaccinations, temperament, etc.). What matters most, however, is your comfort level with the staff. If you get a bad feeling, pay attention to it. After all, you must trust these people with your beloved pet.

built-in doors. Offering your dog full visibility of his surroundings, an x-pen is an ideal spot for your pet when you cannot watch him every moment but you want him to enjoy some fresh air.

Food and Water Bowls

Having an idea of what kind of food and water bowls you want for your Bulldog before heading out to the pet supply store can make the selection task a considerably easier one. There are countless choices available to you, but this needn't be as difficult a decision as it may seem when you round the corner of the feeding accessories aisle.

The three basic varieties you will find there are stainless steel, ceramic, and plastic. My favorite choice by far is flat-bottomed stainless steel for several reasons. It is the most durable, poses no inherent health risks to your pet, and goes with virtually every kind of household décor. I recommend buying four bowls in all, so you always have a clean set ready when the other set is in the dishwasher or when you are heading out to the backyard for a play session.

While ceramic bowls are often more ornate, they can pose a serious threat to your dog in the form of lead. Ceramic products intended for human use are now held to stringent standards to prevent lead poisoning, but the world of canine products has yet to establish similar criteria for ceramic

SENIOR DOG TIP

Build a Routine

If you've adopted an older dog, one way to make him feel more secure is to teach him that he can rely on a regular routine. Feed him at the same times every day, and let him exercise at the same times daily, as well. Establish a regular bed time every night as well. As your pet learns to anticipate the activities of his daily life, he'll come to feel confident in his new home. *(Courtesy of the AAHA and Healthypet.com)*

pottery. If you decide you must have ceramic bowls the same color as your kitchen, consider looking in the housewares section of your favorite department store instead. The dishes found there should be labeled "high fire" or "table quality" and will be safer for your Bulldog. Do bear in mind, though, that a ceramic dish that matches your tile floor perfectly will be no less resistant to shattering if dropped on it.

Plastic dishes pose a different kind of threat to your dog's health—a condition called plastic dish nasal dermatitis. Caused by an antioxidant found in plastic, this contact dermatitis can cause your dog to lose the dark pigmentation in his nose and lips. It can also cause swelling and irritation. Additionally, plastic is considerably more susceptible to being destroyed by a teething puppy, so consider both these facts before purchasing your dog's dishes. If you do opt for plastic, though, be sure the set you select is dishwasher safe, as this will save you time and effort—and allow you to scald away any nasty germs that accumulate on the bowls' surface.

Gate

If, like mine, your home is a little too small to set up an x-pen in your living room, consider investing in one or more safety gates. By using one of these smaller structures, you can transform any pet-proofed room into a safety zone for your Bulldog. This may be especially helpful when you are cleaning up housetraining accidents or if you decide not to crate train your new dog.

At one time, gates were sold exclusively for human babies and toddlers, but you can now find them in both the children's department

and the pet section of most stores. Either should work equally well for your Bulldog, but those found in the doggie aisle may be more resistant to chewing. Some are portable, making it possible for pet owners to use them whenever and wherever they may be helpful. Swing-style models can be mounted to walls or woodwork, allowing household members to conveniently walk through whenever necessary. Like many other canine accessories, gates are offered in a wide array of styles and sizes. The most important consideration is choosing one that is sturdy and safe once put into place. Although accordion-style models are widely available, I discourage pet owners from purchasing these, as they pose a strangulation hazard.

A baby gate comes in handy if you decide not to crate train your dog.

Grooming Supplies

Unlike longer-haired breeds, the Bulldog doesn't require a long list of grooming tools. The things he does need, though, are essential to keeping him looking and feeling his best. Fortunately, none are expensive, and most should last you many years.

Brushes

The first two grooming tools any Bulldog owner needs are a soft-bristled brush and a metal flea comb. Skip the slicker brushes and other harsher instruments designed to untangle minor snarls, as your Bulldog will never have any. Do make sure the brush is stiff enough to reach the skin, though. Plastic combs are cheaper than metal, but the minimal extra amount you will pay for metal will be worth it over time, since you probably won't ever have to replace it.

Nail Clippers

Since your dog's nails should be trimmed every two to three weeks, you will also need a good pair of toenail clippers. These need not be expensive, but they should be the right size and style for your Bulldog. Many owners of large dogs find guillotine-style clippers difficult to maneuver, as the nail itself must be placed inside the guide hole before snipping it. Even with larger clippers, this can be challenging. Scissors-style clippers can also be problematic. While this design can

FAMILY-FRIENDLY TIP

Adult Supervision Required

No matter how mature or dependable your son or daughter may be, it is imperative that the care of your Bulldog not rest solely on the shoulders of a child. Owning a dog is an awesome responsibility, one that few kids can handle without at least some adult supervision. Sharing your Bulldog's care with your child, however, is an excellent way to teach him or her about proper pet care.

Make a list of all the things that must be done for your dog on a daily or weekly basis, and post it where everyone in your household can see it. Encourage your child to assume one or more of these jobs and then check each one off once it has been done, but always follow up to make sure the task has indeed been completed.

sometimes be used on dogs, scissors typically worst best on smaller breeds. The best option for a larger dog like the Bulldog is usually a pliers-style clipper. Resembling a small pair of pruning shears, these clippers allow maximum visibility of the area you are cutting and generally work effectively even on thick nails. Whatever style you

You will also need ear cleanser and canine toothpaste. A toothbrush is optional if you don't mind restocking your dog's grooming bag with gauze from time to time. I find that my own dogs tolerate this impromptu brushing medium much better than the brushes designed specifically for dogs.

Identification

If your dog is ever lost, an identification tag could mean the difference between getting him back or not. Although a dog license bears a unique number that can confirm your dog's identity, an additional tag bearing your name and contact information can enable anyone who may find your Bulldog to return him to you at once. These tags have become extremely inexpensive and accessible. Most national pet store chains have user-friendly machines that custom-engrave a tag with your dog's name and your own, as well as your address and phone number.

If your pet is ever stolen, though, an ID tag will usually be the first thing the perpetrator tosses. In this kind of situation, you will need a more permanent form of identification. At one time, tattoos were the best means of permanently identifying an animal, but as many owners have realized the hard way, even this seemingly indelible mark can be altered. A better option is microchipping your pet.

Making It Legal

In addition to providing your dog with a unique identification number in the event that he is ever lost, dog licenses are also required by law. Although fees are nominal, you will pay even less to register your dog if your Bulldog has been spayed or neutered. (Remember to bring written proof from your veterinarian.) Check with your local municipality for individual prices and other necessary documents you may need to provide during the licensing process.

choose, make sure you select a heavy-duty trimmer, and make sure to keep it sharp. For guillotine-style clippers, this means replacing the blade regularly. For scissors- or pliers-style trimmers, routine sharpening will be necessary. And don't forget to pick up a container of styptic powder to stash in your medicine cabinet—just in case you accidentally cut the quick!

Other Items

Finally, you will need to purchase a few disposable items to meet your Bulldog's grooming needs. A quality shampoo and conditioner top this list.

Microchip

Inserted under your Bulldog's skin in a procedure as quick and painless as a vaccination, a microchip is literally the size of a grain of rice. This small safeguard can make a huge difference in the lives of you and your dog. When read by a handheld device (used by most veterinarians and shelters), the chip provides all the necessary information to lead that person (and your dog) back to you. This indispensable technology has reunited countless pets with their beloved owners—and thwarted a considerable number of animal thefts since its introduction to the pet community.

Of course, no form of identification is useful unless it is used properly. So be sure to attach your dog's new tag to his collar immediately (and securely), and don't forget to register your dog's microchip with the appropriate company. You must also update these records whenever you move or change phone numbers. Always having up-to-

Give your Bulldog plenty of fun, safe toys to play with.

date photos of your dog (especially ones that showcase any distinguishing marks) can also be extremely helpful if your dog is ever lost or stolen.

Leash

Leather leashes wear best, but nylon also works well for most dogs. Extendable leashes are an excellent option if you take regular walks with your dog. If you use a conventional leash, it should afford your Bulldog enough room to walk safely alongside you without his feeling restrictively tethered.

One advantage of using an extendable leash is that it mimics the freedom of running free, allowing your dog to explore his

How Far Should I Walk My Dog?

Question: How far should I walk my dog? I want to make sure my dog gets enough exercise, but I don't want to overexert him. How long should a good walk be for a dog? Does it depend on the dog's size?

Answer: There is not one single right answer to this question. Some dogs will do fine with a two-block walk, while others can go two miles. A good rule of thumb is that the shorter the dog's legs, the less distance he can go. Smaller dogs, like Pugs or other toy breeds, won't be able to go as far as large dogs, like Golden Retrievers. A dog's breed is important as well. Short-legged breeds, like Bulldogs and Dachshunds, won't be able to walk as far as breeds with longer-legged builds. The walking environment is also a factor. Hot weather will not only make a dog more prone to overheating, but it can heat up cement enough that it could be painful for your dog's paws. Dogs can also walk farther on dirt trails than on sidewalks or asphalt, because rough concrete can be hard on the pads of their feet.

Your dog's age and general health are important as well. If your dog doesn't usually get much exercise, you won't want to start him off with a three-mile jog. Gradually extend the length of your walks to build his endurance. Arthritis, heart disease, and a number of other health concerns could also affect the length of your walks. If your dog has health problems, discuss with your veterinarian how far he should walk and how much exercise he should get.

In the long run, your best bet is to observe your dog while you're walking. When he starts panting excessively and acts tired, then he has walked far enough. This is also a good way to keep an eye on your dog's health. If he used to go three miles with you and now can walk only a few blocks, you should consult your veterinarian. It could be a sign of a health problem.

(Courtesy of the AAHA and Healthypet.com)

outdoor surroundings without being placed in harm's way. You must always remain vigilant when walking your dog and shorten the line when walking in higher-traffic areas, but using this kind of lead is like having several different leashes in one. Extendables are also quite handy when training your dog to come when called, as you can let him venture out a bit while still retaining control over his compliance of the command.

Toys

Like children, dogs need toys. They stimulate the brain, provide wonderful opportunities for exercise, and perhaps most important, are just plain fun for your pet. The majority of your Bulldog's toys should be interactive. Whenever you introduce a new toy, begin by showing your dog how to play with it. Roll or bounce a ball, and encourage him to run after it and return it to you. Buy scented tennis balls or flavored bones. And never underestimate the power of a squeaker—dogs, particularly puppies, love things that make noise. After all, part of playtime means being able to be loud and spontaneous.

Chapter **3**

Good
Eating

In an ideal world, we would all simply eat the foods
that are best for us—and only those foods, at least
most of the time. In the real world, achieving a
balanced diet for both people and pets can be a bit
more difficult. In addition to facing the temptations
to overeat and indulge in less-than-healthy choices,
we often just don't know which choice is best. Should
we feed our dogs a premium-brand kibble or a
homecooked regimen? Do our dogs need vitamin
supplements? Should we leave food available to our
pets at all times, or feed them on a schedule?

What makes all these decisions even more complicated is that there are no universal answers.

What works best for one dog may pose a problem for another. There is, however, a wealth of information available to help you make the best decisions for your Bulldog.

Essential Nutrients

A dog's dietary requirements are amazingly similar to the nutrients our own human bodies need. Like us, our dogs need a certain amount of protein, fat, and vitamins. The biggest difference lies in the amount of each nutrient necessary to keep us our healthiest.

Water

The first step in providing your Bulldog with proper nutrition is undoubtedly the easiest. Make sure your dog is given unlimited access to fresh, clean water. This simple task will help maintain a normal body temperature, transport vital nutrients throughout the body, and help eliminate undesired substances in the form of urine.

Your dog needs water regardless of where he is, so always take some along wherever you go. A simple metal bowl and a hose is all you need to keep your

Bulldog from getting dehydrated while playing in the backyard. If you take your dog hiking or for long walks, you can purchase a collapsible bowl that can be filled during a rest period and tucked away when not in use.

Protein

Found in such foods as meat, fish, eggs, milk, and legumes, protein is essential for the growth and repair of body tissue. It also helps maintain the framework that holds the calcium in your dog's bones and teeth. Protein even helps produce antibodies, your dog's best defense against bacteria, viruses, and toxic substances.

Carbohydrates

Although we have been virtually programmed in recent years to think of carbohydrates as a bad thing, they are a common part of many commercial pet foods. An excellent source of calories, carbs serve as an efficient

A balanced diet is essential to your Bulldog's health.

Making Sense of Food Labels

Deciphering food labels can be a confusing undertaking, but armed with a little knowledge, even a novice dog owner can make sense of the information on the back of a food package. Manufacturers are required, to list their physical address on their packaging. Although not legally required, the manufacturer's phone number or website address is preferred. This helps ensure that any additional questions you may have can be answered easily. It also suggests that the company makes customer service a priority.

Once you've located the company's contact information, you will then want to look for another important number—the food's manufacture date. Different companies use different codes for this date, but one of the most popular methods is assigning a four-digit code. The first three digits stand for days of the year and the last digit designates the year. For example, if the code read 0017, 001 stands for the first day of January, and the 7 designates the year 2007.

When stored in a tightly sealed bag or other container, you can expect dry kibble to remain fresh for up to several months. The shelf life of canned food is approximately two years, but once opened it must be stored in the refrigerator and eaten within two or three days. For the sake of simplicity, some dog food brands utilize more-mainstream expiration dates instead.

Although preservatives in general have a negative connotation, the simple truth is that without them, food cannot be kept fresh. Foods preserved with tocopherols have a considerably shorter shelf life than those containing synthetic preservatives, but these vitamin-based preservatives offer more benefits than liabilities. Many consumers try to avoid foods containing butylated hydroxyanisole (BHA), butylated hydroxytoluene (BHT), and ethoxyquin due to claims that these artificial preservatives can cause a number of negative afflictions.

Next, evaluate the ingredients list. This is another often-confusing aspect of reading a dog food label. While the law states that ingredients must be listed in descending order by weight, some companies have found insidious ways around providing full disclosure. By dividing similar ingredients (such as various types of grain) into multiple subcategories, less prominent ingredients can then be boosted to the top of the list. For instance, at first glance a particular food may list chicken as its first ingredient, but the total amount of rice can be listed individually as rice flour and rice gluten, reducing their weight and thus pushing them both further down the line. So while you might think your dog is eating chicken and rice, he may instead be eating rice and chicken.

source of energy. Although they are not technically required in a canine diet, carbohydrates aid in digestion, therefore serving an important role in your Bulldog's dietary plan.

Puppies should be fed more frequently than adults.

Fats

Fats have also gotten a bad rap from us humans, but they are also surprisingly important to your Bulldog. Dogs convert fat into energy at an impressive rate—within just hours— rather than storing it like people do. If your dog doesn't exercise regularly, he will be more likely to gain weight, but even a couch potato pooch will require a higher percentage of fat in his diet than his human counterparts.

Vitamins and Minerals

Vitamins and minerals are given a whole lot of lip service, but rarely do we hear which ones our dogs should be getting. The primary canine vitamins are A, D, E, B complex, and K. If you have any trouble remembering these, just think of this phrase: *A Dog Enjoys Being Kind*. If feeding a prepackaged food, look for these vitamins on the food label, or you can feed fresh foods such as liver, fish, green leafy vegetables, and egg yolks, which contain an ample amount of these vitamins.

Calcium

Calcium is one of the most important minerals for dogs of all ages. In addition to helping maintain strong bones and teeth, calcium is also responsible for certain nerve functions. If your Bulldog's calcium intake is too low, this can increase his risk of joint problems. Most dairy products offer a significant amount of calcium, but some dogs have a hard time digesting these foods. Fortunately, calcium can also be found in vegetables such as broccoli, sweet potatoes, and leafy greens—all practical alternatives for dairy-intolerant canines.

What to Avoid

Perhaps the more important information is which vitamins you should not give your Bulldog. These include supplemental vitamin C—ascorbic acid, sodium ascorbate, calcium ascorbate, and ascorbal palmitate, as these can cause damage to your dog's liver and kidneys.

How Much Should I Feed My Bulldog?

From 8 weeks to 4 months of age	From 3 months to 1 year of age	Adult dogs: 1-2 years and older	Seniors: 6-7 years and older
Bulldog puppies should be placed on a high-quality, medium-breed puppy formula. During this time, the recommended daily serving (look on the back of the package for amount) should be divided into 3–4 meals per day.	At 3 months, your Bulldog should transition from eating 3–4 meals each day to only 2–3 meals per day. This is a good time to evaluate your dog's progress. If he has been gaining an adequate amount of weight, this is a good time to make the switch to adult food to avoid further weight gain from the extra fat and calories of a puppy formula.	As your Bulldog enters adulthood, your choice of food should be based upon several factors—his overall health and condition, energy level, and weight. A weight-maintenance formula may now be the best match for his slightly slower metabolism, especially if his activity level has slowed over the last year.	Now is the time to swap your Bulldog over to a senior diet. Consider feeding a small-bite variety if you feed kibble, since the tinier pieces will be kinder to his mouth if he has any broken or missing teeth. If dry food no longer whets your dog's appetite, instead try offering canned food, which is also available in senior form.

Supplements

If your Bulldog is in good health and eating a well-balanced diet, vitamins and mineral supplements should not be required. When given indiscriminately, in fact, many can be dangerous. If you think your dog may benefit from a particular supplement, talk with your veterinarian before offering it. The best way to offer any vitamin or mineral is in the form of a food containing it, so make the selection of your dog's everyday diet your first priority.

Interestingly, foods containing vitamin E have been shown to help fight cancer in human patients, but this property appears absent when given in supplement form. And remember that sometimes nutrients are provided in unexpected ways. Vitamin D, for example, is found in sunshine.

Although vitamin A is necessary for preventing eye and skin problems, it can be toxic when given in excess. Selenium, while beneficial to the canine heart, can also be toxic when given in doses disproportionate to your dog's weight.

Abstain from offering vitamins or minerals in supplement form unless your veterinarian recommends them. This may be the case if your Bulldog has entered his geriatric years or if he is suffering from an illness. If your dog is young and healthy, however, a well-balanced diet should provide all the nutrients his body needs—without the danger of consuming too much of any one in particular.

Owners must exercise caution even when providing vitamins by way of fresh foods. While the excess amount of a water-soluble vitamin usually passes through your dog's system, fat-soluble vitamins can be stored and build up within your Bulldog's body, unnoticed until they have already caused a problem. Feeding in moderation is always best. Too much of anything can be bad, even if it's a healthy food.

Commercial Foods

With so many canine authorities touting the benefits of raw food or cooking for your pet, you may wonder if feeding your Bulldog a prepackaged food will hurt him. Again, there is no single option that is right for every dog. Many Bulldogs thrive on these more tailor-made diets, but commercial diets also have their benefits. The best food isn't always the most expensive one, but generally speaking, cheap foods are worth what you pay for them. You will find the highest-quality commercial foods in the aisles of your favorite pet supply store. So skip the grocery store if you go this route.

Dry (Kibble)

Dry kibble is the most common prepackaged food choice among dog owners, and the reasons are numerous. It's extremely easy to feed—simply measure and serve twice daily. It works equally well for dogs on either a scheduled or a free-feeding routine, and it can be purchased in bulk and stored with relative ease. Due to its hard and crunchy composition, it also helps keep your Bulldog's teeth clean and free of tartar.

If, like so many other owners, you decide to feed your dog dry food, still more choices await you in the aisles of your local pet supply store. Among these specialized formulas are diets designed especially for high-energy, overweight, and tartar-prone animals. There are even vegetarian options.

Which one is best for your dog will, of course, depend on his individual needs. To provide a unique variety of benefits and tastes, try mixing two different dry foods together. Some canine nutritionists even recommend alternating between several different brands or formulas every few months to ensure that your dog is eating a varied diet that meets all his nutritional needs.

Canned

Like dry dog food, canned food also has its advantages. An older dog with loose or missing teeth, for example, may find wet food easier to chew and generally more appetizing than its less aromatic, dry equivalent. Also like kibble, canned food is easy to prepare, and it can be stored in bulk for a similar time period. Once it is opened, however, wet food must be refrigerated and will keep for only a few days. It is also considerably worse for teeth than kibble is, so keep the canine toothpaste handy if you choose this medium.

Semimoist

Semimoist food may at first seem like the perfect compromise between wet and dry foods, but unfortunately, what is compromised most often

Healthy Rewards

One of the most important things to remember about treats is that they need not always be edible. Treating your pet can sometimes mean taking him for an unexpected walk or play session in the backyard. It can mean taking him along for the ride to return that movie you rented last night. It can even mean planning a playdate with a friend's dog—everyone enjoys spending time with friends, right? Of course, some treats are edible, but this doesn't mean they cannot be healthy. You will likely never have to play airplane to get your Bulldog to eat his veggies. Most dogs will devour carrots and celery as quickly as humans gulp down burgers and fries.

as individual ingredients can vary from one manufacturer to another.

Noncommercial Options

In addition to prepackaged foods, there are also noncommercial feeding options.

Homecooked Diet

One way to make sure you are providing your Bulldog with the best possible nutrition is by feeding him a homecooked diet. This old-fashioned regimen has evolved from the casual practice of tossing the dog the family's leftovers to the careful selection of meats and vegetables prepared especially for your beloved canine. Of course, there will be times when both you and your dog enjoy identical entrées, but homecooking also means keeping abreast of the latest information on what is and isn't best for dogs and adjusting his menus accordingly. For example, garlic can be a healthy ingredient in your Bulldog's meals when used in moderation, but since this vegetable is a member of the onion family (and onions are highly toxic to dogs), your grandmother's spaghetti sauce recipe may not be the best choice for him. Instead, you may be finding yourself making him a more canine-

with this medium is the dog's nutrition. Commonly sculpted into attractive burger shapes, these cute little packages contain an alarming amount of sugar. In addition to being a detriment to your Bulldog's dental health, this also poses an added risk for conditions such as diabetes and will unavoidably lead to obesity, a risk factor for diabetes and a host of other afflictions.

A healthier alternative to most semimoist foods is something called a dog food roll. Packaged similar to salamis, this medium offers a healthy balance of enticing taste and sound nutrition. Do check those labels, though, friendly version of the dish—or something else entirely. Being highly adaptable in this way is integral to a successful homecooking plan.

Pros and Cons

While it's true that you may have to adjust your recipes for your Bulldog, you may also find that adding less (or no) salt is a healthy change for you and the rest of your family, too. Another advantage of homecooking is that you have the flexibility of shopping for your butcher's or grocery store's weekly sales—a harder thing to come by when buying the same package of kibble week after week. Sure, feeding your dog sirloin and salmon may be pricey, but unlike dog food, the price of these items tends to fluctuate much more dramatically.

The biggest disadvantage of homecooking is that dogs on this kind of diet tend to need more frequent dental care. Certainly, feeding harder foods such as raw vegetables will help clean your dog's teeth, but the softer foods have an uncanny ability of calcifying remarkably quickly, particularly on the areas where your Bulldog's teeth meet his gums. This makes the task of brushing daily a near necessity. When started young, this should not be a difficult task, but the level of an owner's dedication to it can mean the difference between sparkling pearly whites and the inevitable reality of decay and tooth loss down the road.

If you realistically do not have time for this vital chore, it may be better to feed your dog a high-quality prepackaged food instead.

Supplementing

If you like the idea of homecooking but do not wish to do it exclusively, an option is to supplement dog food with certain healthy, homecooked choices. Of course, this can be done the opposite way, as well—using the kibble as the supplement. In either case, staying on

FAMILY-FRIENDLY TIP

An Opportunity for Learning

Children of almost any age can participate in feeding a Bulldog. If your son or daughter is especially young, this may mean doing something as simple as carrying a dish or food can. An older child may be trusted to remember the times of day your dog eats or to make sure he always has fresh water in his bowl. The more you involve kids in caring for a pet, the more they learn about proper pet care. Don't be surprised if you catch your 12-year-old reading food labels in the pet supply store and suggesting changes that just may benefit your Bulldog's health!

Good Eating

top of your dog's dental care will still need to be a higher priority than if you were feeding a prepackaged diet alone.

Finally, if you decide that the mainstay of your dog's diet will be coming from homecooked foods, be sure to check with your veterinarian to make sure you have all your dog's nutritional bases covered. All the benefits of a program like this one can easily be sacrificed if your dog is missing out on a crucial vitamin or other dietary necessity. Likewise, an overabundance of a specific ingredient may be just as dangerous as a deficiency. Achieving just the right mix can be a complicated balancing act, but getting this kind of plan right can provide your dog with excellent nutrition—and perhaps just as important, a delightful variety of all his favorite foods.

Raw Diet

Often called the BARF diet (an acronym for *bones and raw food* or *biologically appropriate raw foods*), a raw diet offers dogs the powerful benefits of the vitamins and minerals that are often lost during the cooking process. Additionally, raw foods by definition lack the preservatives that many prepared foods are laden with, and common canine allergens can easily be avoided through careful menu selection.

Although some breeders and veterinarians tout the genuine advantages of a raw diet, most do not give equal candor to the very real liabilities of this risky regimen. Bones, in particular, cause a considerable threat. Chicken bones, for example, pose a substantial choking hazard and are especially prone to splintering—another fact that can have lethal consequences if one of these shards becomes lodged in your Bulldog's intestinal tract. When dealing with raw meat, there is also the deadly threat of bacteria such as salmonella and E. coli. Though frequently overlooked when weighing the pros and cons of a raw diet, these common microorganisms can be just as disastrous to our dogs as they can be to us.

Bulldogs are notorious chow hounds, so don't leave anything out that you don't want eaten.

Safety

The best way to utilize the benefits of a raw diet while not subjecting your Bulldog to the obvious downfalls of this type of plan is to feed raw fruits and vegetables in addition to either a prepackaged or homecooked regimen. Bear in mind, though, that you must blend certain fresh foods in order to reap their benefits. Raw carrots, for example, must be blended before serving so your dog will benefit from the enzyme within this vegetable that is so useful to his health. Most dogs simply don't chew their food enough to accomplish this on their own.

Many raw meals (made either with or without meat) can also be purchased frozen and kept this way until you are ready to serve them, making spoilage a nonissue. This allows owners who feed raw food to buy in bulk. Most important, be especially vigilant if you do choose to feed raw meats, bones (especially when fully cooked), or eggs.

Free Feeding Versus Scheduled Feeding

The choice of whether to schedule your dog's meals or practice free feeding (leaving food available at all times) is probably one of the most individualized decisions a dog owner will make. Either option is acceptable, providing you take your dog's personality into proper consideration. Perhaps your dog, like mine, is unable to pace himself when it comes to eating. If this is the case, free feeding will

Mister Manners

By giving in to begging, you teach your Bulldog that this is an acceptable and effective way of getting what he wants. Does this mean you can never share your favorite edibles with your dog? Not at all. While your dog's diet should consist mainly of healthy food selected especially for him, there is nothing wrong with allowing him an occasional sampling of your own food, as long as you heed a few basic guidelines.

First, never give your dog any food that may be harmful to his health. Chocolate, onions, and macadamia nuts are just a few of the foods dogs should never eat. Next, even healthy foods should be offered in moderation only. Eating too much of anything can cause your Bulldog to gain unnecessary weight and even become sick. Finally, always place your dog's share of whatever you are eating into his dish at the counter, never at the table. By giving your Bulldog food directly from your plate, you blur the lines of what is and isn't acceptable. Instead of allowing sharing to become a bad habit, use it as an opportunity to create good table manners.

If you can't feel your dog's ribs, he's probably overweight.

be out of the question for him. If, however, your Bulldog tends to be a slow eater and appears to prefer returning to his dish throughout the day to munch on a bit of kibble here and there, then free feeding may suit him just fine. The biggest advantage of free feeding is convenience, but make no mistake, there is nothing convenient about the extra pounds your dog will gain from being able to eat as much as he wants. If your dog has trouble knowing when to say when, scheduling is the better option. Unless you plan to supplement your dog's daily food servings (which will inevitably lead to weight gain), he could end up suffering from low blood sugar by the end of the day if he is consuming his entire daily ration each morning.

Another clear disadvantage of free feeding is that you will not know exactly how much your dog is eating if there are multiple pets within your household. In the event that your dog becomes ill, knowing how his appetite has been affected can be vital to diagnosing the problem. If you choose to free feed, you will also be forced to place your dog on a dry food diet. While this may be your choice anyway, it is extremely important that you do not feed fresh, cooked, or canned foods if you plan to leave a full dish out at all times. This could cause the food to spoil and your dog to become sick.

If one method must be identified as the better choice, most would agree that it is using a schedule. Scheduled feedings offer the innate benefit of easier housetraining, because they provide owners with a much better idea of when their dogs need to be taken to their elimination spots. Since it can take some time to determine your new dog's eating style, you may want to begin with a schedule and see how it goes. You can always swap him over to a free-feeding plan, but it can be enormously challenging to transition a dog accustomed to eating whenever he pleases to a more predictable schedule.

Obesity

While food can be an enjoyable part of your Bulldog's healthy lifestyle, it can conversely lead your dog down a road to heart disease, diabetes, and countless other serious health problems. With his thickset appearance, it is easy to see how just a few extra pounds can quickly turn your stout companion into an obese bruiser who becomes winded after just a short walk. With many other breeds, extra weight is usually obvious to an owner's watchful eye, but because of the Bulldog's barrel-shape, a weight problem can easily be overlooked until it becomes a more serious one. A better approach is keeping your finger on the pulse—or more literally, on your dog's ribs. When placing your hands across your dog's chest, his ribs should be discernable, but not prominent. If you must work to find them, there is too much body fat present.

Since this breed is known for its chowhound tendencies, keeping a watchful eye on your dog's diet is the best way to ensure that he remains as fit and trim as possible. This means selecting a diet that provides him with the right balance of nutrients and calories for his particular size and keeping foods that are high in fat and calories to a minimum. When totaling calories, don't forget treats—they count, too! Surprisingly, the total calories in just a few biscuits a day can surpass the calories of a full serving of kibble. An excellent way to treat your dog just as often without the addition of unnecessary weight is breaking each biscuit in half (or

SENIOR DOG TIP

The Senior Menu

Many older dogs benefit from specially formulated food that is designed with older bodies in mind. Obesity in pets is often the result of reduced exercise and overfeeding and is a risk factor for problems such as heart disease. Because older dogs often have different nutritional requirements, these special foods can help keep your pet's weight under control and reduce consumption of nutrients that are risk factors for the development of diseases, as well as organ and age-related changes. *(Courtesy of the AAHA and Healthypet.com)*

thirds, depending on its size) before offering it to your dog.

Of course, exercise also plays an important role in keeping your dog from becoming overweight, but owners must be careful that they keep their expectations reasonable. Since this breed is prone to breathing difficulties and hip problems, exercise must be regular but moderate in nature. This is not a dog you should take along with you on your morning run.

Chapter 4

Looking Good

"A healthy Bulldog is a beautiful thing," says Nancy Rose, DVM. Of all the things that make this unique breed so appealing, it is proper care that makes him both look and feel his best. Certainly, there are numerous breeds with more-elaborate grooming needs, but grooming your Bulldog is no less important because it takes less time. In fact, the ease of keeping him clean and coiffed makes your commitment to these tasks even more essential.

Whether you are bringing home a Bulldog puppy or you have adopted an older dog, there is no reason to postpone grooming. Even if you have already begun to let things slide, the longer you continue putting it off, the harder it will be to establish a grooming schedule. The best time for grooming is now. By exposing your dog to brushing and bathing and toenail clipping as early as possible, you will help him tolerate all these tasks much better. You just may find that he even starts to enjoy some of them.

Coat and Skin Care
Your Bulldog's short coat is easy to groom, but it still needs attention.

Brushing
When most people think of brushing, images of long-haired dogs immediately spring to mind: Cocker Spaniels, Lhasa Apsos, Afghan Hounds. While unsnarling knots is an important part of the process for these breeds, an equally important albeit overlooked reason to brush any dog is for removing dead hair and dirt from his coat. Yes, even short-haired dogs shed, and by making brushing a routine grooming task, you will lessen the amount of hair left on your floor, furniture, and clothing.

Brushing also helps remove any toxic substances that your dog has unknowingly picked up during his walks around the neighborhood. Lawn treatments, de-icing agents, and a plethora of other chemicals are lurking virtually everywhere. Since your Bulldog licks his paws daily as part of his self-grooming routine, he is also ingesting this matter that repeatedly becomes embedded in his coat. For this important reason, frequent brushing is a smart idea even though your Bulldog's hair won't knot like that of many other breeds.

How to Brush Your Bulldog
Unlike the owners of those fluffier canines, you won't need a Master's degree in brushing to keep your Bulldog properly primped. You won't even have to learn any fancy techniques. Whenever time allows,

Necessary Gadgets
Your dog's grooming bag needn't be big, but there are a few items that every Bulldog needs:
- A soft-bristled brush and metal flea comb
- Moisturizing shampoo
- Nail clippers
- Ear cleaning solution
- Canine toothpaste and toothbrush (or gauze)
- Medicated powder with menthol and zinc oxide
- Panalog ointment (an anti-inflammatory, antifungal, and antibacterial veterinary ointment)

simply brush your dog's hair gently, using a soft-bristled brush. If he shows any aversion to the process, begin instead by simply using your fingers, gently massaging him in a series of brushing motions. Most dogs learn quickly that brushing feels great, so transitioning to a real brush shouldn't be difficult.

Combing is the typical way to finish off a brushing session. For other breeds, this is primarily to make sure that no tangles or mats have been missed. In your Bulldog's case, however, the flea comb will have a literal purpose: to make sure that none of those pesky little creatures are waiting to assault your precious pet.

Bathing

The second part to keeping your Bulldog's hair and skin clean and healthy is regular bathing. This doesn't mean giving your dog a weekly bath but rather cleaning the most-problematic areas—such as his many wrinkles—about once a week and scheduling full baths approximately every two to three weeks. If your dog's wrinkles are especially prone to accumulating dirt and bacteria, it may be necessary to apply powder or

How Often Should I Clean My Bulldogs Wrinkles?

When your Bulldog is a puppy, you may need to clean his wrinkles only once a week. As he gets older, though, this job will need to be done more often—perhaps as frequently as daily. Many owners find it handy to keep a container of aloe baby wipes on hand just for this purpose. Be sure to pay special attention to the wrinkles over your dog's nose, on his forehead, around the nose, and under the eyes. Dry each wrinkle completely once you are done cleaning, though, as trapped moisture can harbor bacteria.

ointment to these areas regularly, as well. Your vet should be able to recommend what would be appropriate for your dog's needs.

If you plan to show your Bulldog, you may increase the frequency of bathing to keep him in tip-top shape for the ring, but always use a quality shampoo and be careful to rinse all of it from his coat to avoid unnecessarily drying his skin.

How to Bathe Your Bulldog

Before placing your dog in your bathtub, gently position one cotton ball in each of his ears to prevent water from entering this area. Now your dog is ready for the water. After wetting his coat, pour a small amount of shampoo into your hand and work it into your Bulldog's fur, forming a moderate lather. Your dog's shampoo won't yield the same amount of suds as your own shampoo. This makes it easier for you to rinse it thoroughly from his coat. Always use a quality canine shampoo on your Bulldog— never a product made for humans.

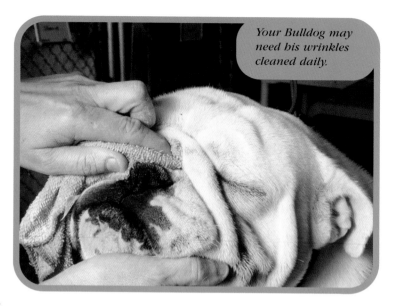

Your Bulldog may need his wrinkles cleaned daily.

Once you have finished washing, drain the tub and start the rinsing process. The best way to ensure proper rinsing is repeating the process several times, even if you feel certain you have already done a thorough job. Even a small amount of suds left in your dog's coat can cause itchy, dry skin.

If you will be using a conditioner, this is the time to apply it—rinsing your dog carefully once again. You may think the only purpose of conditioners is to untangle the hair of long-locked breeds, but conditioners can actually be tremendously helpful

in keeping your Bulldog's shorter hair and skin soft and smooth. There are also specialty versions of shampoos and conditioners available to help with specific problems such as dandruff or skin discoloration.

Next, wet your washcloth and gently wash your dog's face with plain water. When you are done, you can then remove the cotton balls from your Bulldog's ears and gently wipe the insides with mineral water. Drying your dog's wrinkles thoroughly will also help prevent more-serious problems like facial fold dermatitis, a common condition in this breed. Blow drying, while not necessary, can be helpful, especially on colder days. Be sure to use a low-heat setting, though, so you don't burn your pet's sensitive skin.

Nail Care

Although a properly trimmed paw certainly looks great, the bigger reason for performing regular pedicures on your Bulldog is safety—both his and that of others. As soon as you can hear your dog's nails when he walks across the floor, he is already overdue for a trim. Just standing on a foot with long toenails can be painful for your pet. It is his legs and feet that should bear his weight, after all, not his toenails.

Overgrown nails can also rip or tear. This can expose the nail bed, the sensitive area beneath the nail. Even more painful than this is having a nail pulled completely out if it gets caught on something such as clothing or carpeting—an accident that can also leave your Bulldog extremely susceptible to infection. Nails left to grow too long can also scratch; your dog can hurt both himself and other household members with these talonlike claws.

As important as frequent nail trimming is, the task is no less intimidating due its necessity. If you are anything like me, just the prospect of a canine pedicure can make you even more nervous, since cutting into your dog's nail bed (or quick) can hurt your beloved pet. For this very reason, you must force yourself to overcome your fears as soon as possible. Like most things we humans tend to dread, the anticipation is far worse than the task of trimming. So commit to a schedule of weekly nail trims as soon as you bring your Bulldog home. Interestingly, trimming this frequently has actually been shown to make the quick recede over time, thus reducing your chances of accidentally hurting your dog.

Another excellent way to lessen the risk of cutting your dog's quick is helping him become more comfortable with having his paws handled. Whenever the opportunity presents itself, gently massage your Bulldog's

You can use a towel to dry your Bulldog, or a blow dryer for colder days.

feet. This will show him that touch feels good and that he has nothing to fear from having his nails cut. And speaking of fear, do your best to overcome your own. Animals, particularly dogs, are prolific readers of human body language. If you are worried about hurting your dog, he will pick up on it—and shy away from you when it comes time for nail trimming.

How to Trim Your Bulldog's Nails

Place your dog in standing position, holding his foot firmly and pressing gently on the pad to extend the nail. It is easier to see the quick on nails that are light in color, but unfortunately individual dogs frequently have a combination of light and dark-colored nails—sometimes even on the same foot. Using your clippers, snip off just the hook-like end of the nail on a 45-degree angle. Especially if you cannot discern the quick, err on the side of caution.

Continue this method until all the nails on the foot have been trimmed. For a puppy, it may take several days to finish all four feet, but the more often you trim, the more he will get used to having this important job

When trimming your Bulldog's nails, be careful not to cut the quick.

done. Touching your dog's feet at other times will also help get him used to having his feet handled—a huge hurdle in the tolerance factor, so gently massage his paws as often as possible while he's young. Giving in to wiggling or whining by postponing the task will only teach your dog that these tactics work, so be persistent.

If You Cut the Quick

Unfortunately, accidents happen sometimes. If you cut your Bulldog's nails a little too short and nip the quick, don't panic. Apply pressure to area with a clean cloth soaked in water. You may also apply a styptic pencil or powder to stop persistent bleeding. Several household items may be substituted for these items—including cornstarch, a bar of soap, or a wet tea bag.

While the occasional slipup shouldn't damage your dog's tolerance for nail trimming, frequent cuts can have an adverse effect on his comfort level. So if you find yourself repeatedly searching for the styptic powder, consider leaving this task to another family member or a professional groomer. This will make the task easier on both you and your Bulldog.

Ear Care

The most convenient time to clean your Bulldog's ears is when you are bathing him, but this is not the only time the task should be performed. On the contrary, you should be cleaning your dog's ears at least twice for every one bath he is given. It is far easier to prevent an ear infection than it is to treat one, so don't let this simple task slide to the back burner.

How to Clean Your Bulldog's Ears

Begin by squirting a liberal amount of ear cleaner into your dog's ear canal. Be forewarned: Most dogs resist this step. Next, rub the ear from the outside. Your dog will probably lean into your hand at this point, which helps loosen any dirt and debris inside the ear. He may also shake his head, which, though messy, will also help with this loosening process.

Once the ear has been sufficiently lubricated, insert a cotton ball (never a swab) to wipe the inside of the ear. Repeat this step until the cotton comes out mostly clean. Like the human ear canal, a small amount of wax is

Use a cotton ball to clean your Bulldog's ears.

necessary to maintain proper function. Unlike our own, however, the canine ear canal is much less vulnerable to injury. The L-shaped opening can be penetrated safely to the point of the 90-degree turn. You must still be careful, though; a gentle hand is always best.

Select a solution that is free of both alcohol and peroxide, common ingredients in many popular brands. Though effective for cleaning, these ingredients can be harsh on sensitive skin, especially if your dog is already suffering from an infection. If you

suspect that your Bulldog's ear is already infected, check for an offensive odor. A healthy ear should never smell. Refrain from cleaning the ear at this time, though, for doing so will likely further irritate an already tender area and also put your veterinarian at a disadvantage in terms of swabbing the ear to accurately diagnose the problem.

Eye Care

All you must do to keep your Bulldog's peepers looking their best is wipe the area around the eyes with a wet cloth whenever sleep or matter appears. For some dogs, this may be weekly; for others, it may be daily. Allowing this matter to accumulate leaves your dog more prone to infections, such as conjunctivitis (pink eye), and discoloration.

Whenever you wipe your dog's eyes, examine them for any signs of a problem. Scratches, cloudiness, extreme redness, or excessive discharge are all causes for concern and should be addressed with your dog's veterinarian. Any problem that is found early has a better chance of not becoming a more serious issue. For this reason, it is a good preventive measure to have your dog seen by a veterinary ophthalmologist at least once every few years. To locate a canine ophthalmologist in your area, visit the American College of Veterinary Ophthalmologists (ACVO) at www.acvo.com.

FAMILY-FRIENDLY TIP

No Small Matter

Children as young as kindergartners can help with grooming. Of course, five- and six-year-olds aren't old enough to perform more complicated tasks such as cleaning ears or brushing teeth, but they can handle simple jobs like brushing coats and helping with baths. As children get older and are taught more about grooming, they may be trusted with more-intricate tasks. The best way to build trust between your Bulldog and your kids is early involvement, so remember that no task is too small to merit sharing.

Dental Care

There is hardly a grooming task that affects your Bulldog's overall health more than caring for his teeth. Bacteria that are allowed to accumulate in your dog's mouth are ultimately transported throughout his body, exposing his entire physical being to countless afflictions. Dogs suffering from tooth decay or gingivitis are at a considerably higher risk of developing conditions as superficial (albeit unpleasant) as bad breath or as serious as coronary heart disease.

Brushing your dog's teeth may seem like an arduous task, but it is one that you will never regret. This task, which literally takes just minutes a day, can conceivably save your dog's life. But what if you can't manage to do it every single day? Don't despair if this is the case. Just make brushing a priority by getting the job done as often as you can. The worst thing you can do is skip the task entirely because you can't stick to a daily schedule.

If you can't brush your Bulldog's teeth as often as you'd like, consider feeding dry food. This will lessen the amount of calculus (more commonly called tartar) that accumulates on your dog's teeth between your informal cleanings. It will also prolong the need for a professional cleaning, a procedure that requires general anesthesia.

Like all grooming tasks, brushing your dog's teeth will be easier on both you and him if you start the habit while he is

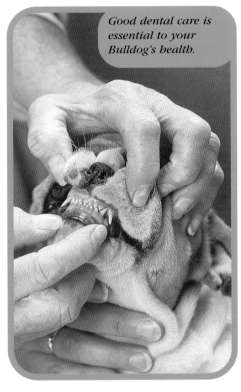

Good dental care is essential to your Bulldog's health.

49

young. The typical tools of the trade are a tube of canine toothpaste and a toothbrush. Although a human's toothbrush can be used, never use your own toothpaste, as this can harm your pet. Many times, a brush is included in the package when you purchase toothpaste made for your dog, but even the brush is not absolutely necessary. You can "brush" your dog's teeth with pieces of white gauze instead.

How to Brush Your Bulldog's Teeth

When you are ready to brush your dog's teeth, always begin by offering

A rugby shirt can ward off chills on a cool day.

him a taste of his toothpaste. Most brands are available in such tempting flavors as chicken, liver, and even bacon. This will help hold his attention and get his mouth open for you to do the important part—the cleaning. Wet the brush or a piece of gauze before you begin, and place a small amount of the toothpaste in its center. Beginning at the gum line, focus on one tooth at a time and start brushing in an oval motion. If you use a conventional brush, hold it at a 45-degree angle. The outside of the upper teeth is usually the area in need of the most attention, but don't forget to reach all 42 teeth (28 if your Bulldog is still a puppy), both front and back. Finish off with a drink. Although rinsing is not necessary, a little water is always a refreshing way to end this important task.

Bulldog Accessories

My husband always snickers at me when I put coats on our dogs. He thinks clothing for dogs is at best unnecessary, at worst absurd. There are, however, some instances where a coat for your dog may be necessary. If you live in an especially cold climate like we do, for instance, your Bulldog's short fur may not always be enough to keep him sufficiently warm— particularly when spending a lengthy amount of time outdoors. If you find cutesy sweaters or jackets emasculating, consider a simple fleece coat. This will provide your dog with the warmth he needs, but it won't hurt his tough-guy image.

Another practical accessory for your Bulldog is paw wax. This amazing product helps protect your dog's paw pads from the burns of hot asphalt and cold ice, so he can walk confidently no matter what the season. It also reduces his risk of slipping—an accident that can land your precious pet in the hospital or even in line for surgery. To provide a layer of protection to your dog's feet, apply paw wax thickly whenever your Bulldog will be walking on any surface that can hurt his feet.

Of course, you can find a plethora of other canine accessories at any pet supply store or online retailer. Which ones are truly worth the investment? The answer depends somewhat on your individual circumstances. Perhaps your Bulldog likes to spend a

SENIOR DOG TIP

Grooming the Older Dog

Grooming an older Bulldog differs from grooming a younger one in two significant ways. First, the tasks will invariably take a little longer as your dog ages, and second, they will become even more important to his overall health. This does not mean you will need to learn how to groom your older dog all over again. You will just have to slow down a bit; watch for any signs of illness or injuries, which are more common in older dogs; and never put off until tomorrow what you can groom today.

considerable amount of time outside, making a citronella bug spray a smart preventive step. Or you may consider taking canine attire to the next level by buying your rain-shy dog a pair of galoshes. The best questions to ask when selecting a product for your dog are these: How will this help my dog? And perhaps even more important, Can it hurt him? If you can't answer the first question, or if you answer yes to the second, you should pass on the item no matter how cute it is.

Looking Good

Chapter 5

Feeling Good

Who's the first person who springs to mind when you think of your Bulldog's health? His veterinarian? His breeder? While both these individuals certainly have a profound effect on your dog's well-being, the person who has the greatest impact on your dog's health is you. As your dog's biggest advocate, you are the one making the decisions that most affect your beloved pet's future.

Everything from your selection of his diet and exercise regimen to your choice of his preventive medications and routine vaccinations can ultimately determine whether your dog is a fit and active companion protected against the threats of disease and injury—or a couch potato prone to a number of debilitating medical conditions. This is an awesome responsibility, to be sure, but one that also empowers an owner with the wondrous potential to lengthen his or her pet's life.

Beginning by selecting a responsible breeder, you will be stacking the odds in your Bulldog's favor that he will live a long and healthy life. If, instead, you adopt or rescue your Bulldog, you will be making a huge difference in the life of a dog who otherwise may never know the joys of sharing his life with a compassionate human in a permanent home. In either case, the next step you take in maintaining your new friend's good health should be finding a veterinarian with whom both you and your dog are comfortable.

Finding a Vet

A long time ago, veterinarians seemed to work geographical territories. If you lived in a certain city or town,

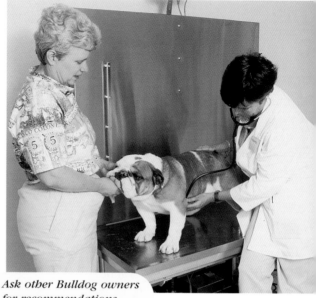

Ask other Bulldog owners for recommendations for veterinarians.

you would most likely use the vet who cared for the animals in that area. Now there are myriad choices of veterinarians and practices almost everywhere. Some specialize in certain areas of veterinary medicine—ophthalmology or orthopedics, for instance—while others offer more-generalized care. Some vets are trained in complementary medicine, while others stick to more conventional forms of treatment. Most will readily work together when beneficial, and regularly refer clients to one another. Just open your phone book, and you will find a plethora of options, probably all within 10 to 15 miles of your home. This growing list of names presents one challenge, though. How do you know which vet is the right one for you and your dog?

The best advice? Steer clear of that phone book, at least initially. Begin instead by asking for recommendations from other dog owners, particularly those who also own Bulldogs. Your breeder and local humane society can also provide you with a solid list of choices.

Although it may at first seem overwhelming, the process of choosing a vet shouldn't be a stressful one. In fact, one of your goals should be keeping the experience as relaxing as possible for your dog, as he will be forming his early impressions of health care as you interview candidates for this job. You can even use his reactions to guide you through the process. Animals are highly intuitive individuals. Many dogs have a natural fear of new places, particularly veterinary hospitals with so many new smells and strangers with their pets, but the staff should forge a good relationship with your dog, so any fear can be minimized. If your Bulldog takes an instant disliking to an individual, pay attention—especially if that person is the veterinarian. A natural rapport with animals (specifically dogs) should be a prerequisite for the job of your dog's vet.

Take a Tour

Begin by phoning the practice you are considering and requesting a tour of the hospital. You may need to wait until a less hectic part of the day

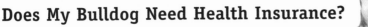

Does My Bulldog Need Health Insurance?

Although the scale is smaller, the cost of canine health care is rising just like the price of our own medical care. In addition to annual vet visits, dog owners should anticipate having their pets spayed or neutered, providing them with regular medications for heartworm and flea and tick prevention, and heading to the vet's office for unexpected problems that occasionally arise. These costs can add up quickly.

A great way to be sure that the costs remain manageable is purchasing health insurance for your Bulldog. Several national companies offer such policies, which reimburse owners for everything from annual visits to prescriptions. Is it worth it? The decision is much like the one you make for your own health insurance. As long as your dog is healthy, this protection may seem like a luxury, but if he ever suffers from a catastrophic illness or injury, you may be glad you have it. Since Bulldogs are prone to so many health problems, you may be very glad. If you are interested in purchasing pet health insurance, ask your vet to recommend a provider.

You and your vet will be partners in keeping your Bulldog healthy.

good to know from the beginning which way the hospital operates rather than to be surprised on a return trip.

Look for clean, well-organized facilities, but not necessarily large spaces filled with expensive equipment. Some of the best veterinarians run modest practices—and by doing so keep their prices equally moderate. Both the veterinarian and his or her support staff should project a positive attitude and seem to enjoy their jobs. A good working knowledge of animal health and behavior is also useful. You mustn't expect the receptionist or veterinary technician (or even the vet, for that matter) to have all the answers, but each of these caregivers should always be willing to help find the answers you seek. Although it may not matter to everyone, I personally find that compassionate employees make a huge difference to owners and dogs alike.

Find out if a staff member is on site at all times. If your dog ever needs to stay overnight, 24-hour care should be provided, especially in the event that he has had surgery and post-operative bleeding may be a concern. Also, ask if there are separate facilities for treating infectious animals. Some vets go as far as to offer separate waiting rooms for sick pets and those visiting for routine care.

or week, but a reputable facility should have no problem with taking you on a guided tour to meet the staff and view the facilities. Nowadays many hospitals have websites offering virtual tours; while these may be helpful, nothing replaces an in-person inspection. Your visit should include an opportunity to meet the veterinarian your dog will be seeing. Remember to ask if this will be the vet who examines your dog each time he is due for a checkup or if the doctors share clients on a rotating schedule. There is no right or wrong answer to this question, but you may have a personal preference. It is also

Other Factors

Other important factors may be the costs of services, your vet's location, and parking. Ask for a price list of common services, and don't forget to inquire about a multiple-pet discount if you have more than one animal. Traveling an extra half hour to a vet you really like may be well worth the trip if your dog is scheduled for a checkup, but you should have an emergency plan in place for more time-sensitive situations. Emergency clinics that are open during conventional vets' off-hours (or even 24 hours a day) are wonderful resources for this purpose.

Your veterinarian will technically be working for you, but never underestimate the importance of your working together for the all-important goal of your dog's physical and mental health. If you make an appointment, show up on time, and bring any samples that were requested. Your expectations should be high but reasonable—and you should always strive to match these expectations yourself as a courteous client.

Your Bulldog's Annual Vet Visit

Initially, your Bulldog puppy will need to visit the veterinarian every few weeks, but once he has received all his necessary shots and boosters, you will need to take him only for a routine exam once a year. At this time, your dog will be weighed and have his temperature taken, and you will be

Your Bulldog's First-Aid Kit

The following items should always be kept on hand in the event of a medical emergency:

- Antibiotic ointment
- Canine first-aid manual
- Children's diphenhydramine (antihistamine)
- Cotton swabs
- Emergency phone numbers (including poison control, an emergency veterinarian, and your dog's regular vet)
- Flashlight
- Hydrogen peroxide
- Instant ice pack
- Ipecac syrup
- Nonstick gauze pads, gauze, and tape
- Oral syringe or eyedropper (plastic, not glass)
- Rectal thermometer
- Saline solution
- Scissors
- Soap
- Styptic powder or pencil
- Tweezers
- Any other item your veterinarian recommends keeping on hand. Remember to keep an eye on expiration dates and toss any products before they should no longer be used.

Feeling Good

asked a number of questions pertaining to his appetite, exercise regimen, and general health and behavior. The veterinary technician often handles this initial interview process, noting any pertinent information in your dog's chart that should be discussed further with the veterinarian.

The vet will then join you and conduct a thorough physical examination of your dog—including his eyes, ears, teeth, heart, lungs, and joints and kneecaps. It may also be time for certain vaccinations. Additionally, this is an ideal opportunity to pick your vet's brain about any questions you may have in relation to your dog's health and well-being. By educating dog owners, your vet makes his or her own job easier, so never hesitate to ask a question no matter how elementary you fear it may be.

Asking Questions

Remember, your veterinarian has a wealth of experience to share with you not only about health-related topics but also pertaining to more-generalized dog care. Having a problem with housetraining regression? Ask for some tips in remedial training. Does your dog suffer from separation anxiety? Mention it! In addition to solving the problem, you just may find a medical component to the issue that you were originally unaware of. There is a

profound relationship between an animal's mind and body. An ideal vet will see your dog as a whole patient with an array of needs and nuances as diverse as a human's.

As tempting as it may be to skip this annual routine visit if your dog always seems to ace his exam, *don't*. This yearly physical can alert you to a number of dangerous conditions before they become larger problems. Dogs are amazingly resilient animals who don't always let us know when they aren't feeling well. We owe it to them to keep an eye on even the smallest changes in their health so we can keep them feeling their best.

Vaccinations

There has been a lot of discussion among pet owners lately about

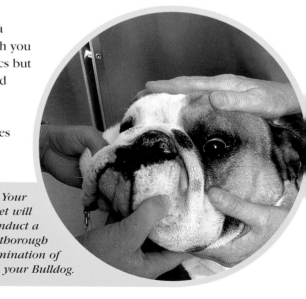

Your vet will conduct a thorough examination of your Bulldog.

vaccinations. Similar to concerns over human vaccinations for children, the issues of when and how often to vaccinate our dogs are complicated ones with few clear right or wrong answers. The most important thing to remember when deciding which vaccines are best for your Bulldog is that most of these choices are up to you. With a couple of exceptions (the rabies vaccine being one of these), most shots are not mandatory by law. This means you can personally consider the most up-to-date information and select the vaccinations you and your veterinarian think are practical for your dog.

One of the problems critics of the vaccination process cite doesn't relate to the vaccines themselves but rather to how often a particular vaccine is administered. This is the reason that most US states now require the rabies vaccine only every three years instead of annually or bi-annually, as was the case just a short time ago. This makes sense, as we do not require people to get annual shots of most vaccines. Instead, we get boosters at more reasonable intervals—or just a single vaccination during childhood. The veterinary community and subsequently our governing bodies are now realizing that a conservative approach is also better for our pets.

Sometimes, though, it is the vaccine itself that poses the health risk. Nearly all vaccinations carry at least some

FAMILY-FRIENDLY TIP

Preparing a Child for What Happens at the Vet

One of the best ways to include your child in your Bulldog's health care is allowing him or her to attend your dog's veterinary checkups. Remember, though, that it can be scary for a young child to visit a veterinary hospital for the first time.

To make things easier on both your dog and your child (remember, anxiety can be contagious), prepare your child for the checkup before exam day arrives. Ask what he or she thinks might happen when your dog visits the vet. Discuss the differences between his or her doctor and a veterinarian. Tell your child that just like he or she doesn't like having shots, your dog may flinch a bit when a needle goes in, but it will be over quickly—and that other tasks (such as getting weighed and having his temperature taken) don't hurt a bit. An especially good veterinarian will explain the things he or she does to both you and your child, so keeping your Bulldog healthy can be a family affair.

59

Feeling Good

possibility of side effects. These may range from negligible to severe. They may also pose a threat only to a certain section of the canine population.

Leptospirosis

Whether a vaccine is advisable for your Bulldog largely depends on his individual risk factors for that particular disease or infection. Leptospirosis, for example, is an organism ingested through the urine passed by infected animals. If your Bulldog is paper-trained or has an enclosed pen to which he is taken to do his daily business, his chance of coming in contact with infected urine is slim. Since a higher risk of side effects—including anaphylaxis—is associated with leptospirosis-containing vaccines, vaccinating wouldn't be prudent in this case. If, however, you live in an area where both your dog and a plethora of wildlife share a backyard, you may want to consider the "lepto" shot. Remember, the animals need not occupy the space simultaneously for a high risk to be present. Many wild animals frequent rural (and even suburban) neighborhoods at night while families and their pets are sleeping.

Parvovirus and Distemper

The dangers of certain diseases, however, far outweigh the risks

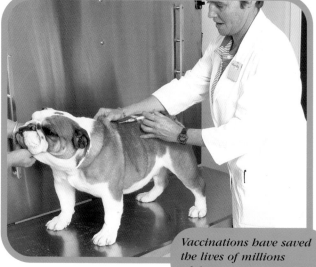

Vaccinations have saved the lives of millions of dogs.

associated with vaccination. Parvovirus is one such affliction. Probably the most common canine viral illness, "parvo" most commonly strikes young dogs, but the consequences can be deadly at any age. Although it is possible that lifelong immunity is obtained through a single successful vaccination (which can be difficult to accomplish in young dogs, since the antibodies passed to puppies from their mothers can actually interfere with the vaccine), there currently is not sufficient evidence to warrant lengthening the time period between this vaccine's annual boosters.

The parvo vaccine is included in a popular combination shot recommended by most veterinarians. The shot includes the vaccine that also protects your dog against distemper,

another serious viral disease that is contagious, incurable, and often fatal.

Combo Shots

The most important thing to remember about combo shots is that one of these should never be administered at the same time as any other vaccination. Although most combinations are considered safe when given by themselves, whenever giving shots the best guideline is the fewer the better. Receiving too many shots at one time can lead to any number of unpleasant side effects—including autoimmune diseases and even death.

It is also vital to remember that no vaccines should ever be given when a dog is ill. This means that your Bulldog's temperature should always be taken before the administering of any shots, as an elevated temperature is a common sign of infection. Once your dog has been fully examined and given a clean bill of health, then and only then should shots be given.

Rabies

The rabies vaccine is mandatory in all 50 US states. As more is being learned, however, many states are extending the length of time for which a

vaccination is considered effective by law. The most important thing to know is that vaccinations were developed for good reasons. Rabies, which leads to acute encephalitis (brain swelling), is a zoonotic disease. This means that it not only affects animals, but it can also be passed to humans. Diseases such as rabies and parvovirus once wiped out entire kennels when they struck, so not vaccinating for these afflictions isn't the answer. At the same time, learning as much as we can about the current protocol—and adjusting our plans accordingly—can only help ensure that our dogs are being protected against both the diseases themselves and any unnecessary side effects from the shots. The rabies vaccine, for instance, was once a yearly requirement, but now only needs to be administered every two or three years in most states. Other vaccines are currently being evaluated in this same way.

Optional Shots

Other common canine shots include the kennel cough (bordetella) and Lyme vaccines. If your Bulldog participates in any organized activity (such as conformation or agility) or if he is taken to a professional groomer or doggie daycare facility, you should

Why Spay or Neuter?

Spaying or Neutering Is Good for Your Pet

- Spaying and neutering help dogs live longer, healthier lives.

- Spaying and neutering can eliminate or reduce the incidence of a number of health problems that can be difficult or expensive to treat.

- Spaying eliminates the possibility of uterine or ovarian cancer and greatly reduces the incidence of breast cancer, particularly when your pet is spayed before her first estrous cycle.

- Neutering eliminates testicular cancer and decreases the incidence of prostate disease.

Spaying or Neutering Is Good for You

- Spaying and neutering make pets better, more affectionate companions.

- Spaying a dog eliminates her heat cycle. Estrus lasts an average of 6 to 12 days, often twice a year. Females in heat can cry incessantly, show nervous behavior, and attract unwanted male animals.

- Unsterilized animals often exhibit more behavior and temperament problems than do those who have been spayed or neutered. Spaying and neutering can make pets less likely to bite. Neutering makes males less likely to get into fights with other animals.

Spaying or Neutering Are Good for the Community

- Communities spend millions of dollars to control unwanted animals.

- Irresponsible breeding contributes to the problem of dog bites and attacks. Animal shelters are overburdened with surplus animals. Stray pets and homeless animals get into trash containers, defecate in public areas or on private lawns, and frighten or anger people who have no understanding of their misery or needs.

- Spay or neuter surgery carries a one-time cost that is relatively small when one considers its benefits. It's a small price to pay for the health of your pet and the prevention of more unwanted animals.

(Courtesy of the Humane Society of the United States)

consider the kennel cough vaccine. Many establishments even require it. If he encounters other canines only occasionally and in low numbers, however, this vaccine probably isn't necessary.

The Lyme vaccine, on the other hand, is recommended for most dogs living in the United States. The risks of this serious disease far outweigh the risk the vaccine may pose. Unlike ticks of other varieties, the deer tick (the carrier of Lyme disease) is so small that most owners can easily overlook it even on a smooth-coated animal. Moreover, once the pinhead-sized tick is discovered, it is often too late—the disease can be transmitted to a healthy dog in just a day or two.

Fleas and Ticks

Fleas

Though not usually thought of as a dangerous problem, flea bites can lead to a number of serious canine health issues. By protecting your dog with a monthly flea and tick preventative, you can easily avoid a painful and exasperating infestation and possibly several other health problems. As with so many other afflictions, it is highly preferable to prevent fleas rather than eliminate them once they have set up residence.

If your pet has already been accosted by fleas, it is imperative that you not only treat him, but that you also treat his entire environment. Fleas reproduce at an astounding rate, leaving entire households vulnerable to the conditions they cause—from anemia to tapeworms. First, wash your pet thoroughly with a flea shampoo. Then, remove all people and pets from your home before you use a flea bomb (or fogger), following the product's directions carefully. Also, be sure to throw away your vacuum cleaner bag. It only takes a single stowaway flea to start a whole new wave of infestation.

Ticks

Lyme disease has quickly become the most notorious tick-related illness in the United States. Whenever outdoors, I am constantly checking my own dogs for the frighteningly small deer ticks that transmit this grave illness. Even with my constant vigilance, though, my

Check your dog for fleas and ticks after he's been outside.

Removing a Tick

If you find a tick on your dog, use a pair of tweezers to carefully remove it. It is vital that you get both the tick's head and body out. Use a pair of sterilized tweezers to grasp the tick's body, and begin pulling it away from your dog's skin very gently. Apply steady pressure, but be sure not to squeeze too tightly. Jiggling the tick a bit is fine, but don't rotate it.

Once the tick is out drop it in some alcohol. Never use your bare hands or feet to kill a tick. As soon as the tick has been properly disposed of, clean the bite wound with disinfectant, and sterilize your tweezers with some fresh alcohol.

If you cannot get the tick to release, or if you remove only part of it, seek assistance from your veterinarian.

dog Damon tested positive for Lyme disease just recently. The scariest part was also the saving grace of the situation. At the time of his test, he showed absolutely no symptoms; this is why regular testing is so important. Without the test, I likely wouldn't have known my dog was ill until he was in much greater danger.

While owners should certainly be on the lookout for this menacing deer tick, we mustn't overlook the other equally treacherous tick varieties that can cause your dog (or your human family members) to become ill. Among the other diseases that ticks can transmit are Rocky Mountain Spotted Fever, encephalitis, tulameria, and tick paralysis. Although ticks are sluggish and incapable of flight, even large ones can be easily overlooked. My own dogs are proof of this. It is why you should always examine your Bulldog thoroughly whenever coming in from the great outdoors.

Breed-Specific Illnesses

The Bulldog is a breed who can suffer from a number of conditions.

Acne

Like human teenagers, Bulldogs experience puberty. Interestingly, this often exposes them to another issue common in humans—acne. Although your dog enters his adolescence between the ages of five and eight months, the rest of the problem is much the same as when acne strikes human patients. Genetics, hormones, and stress may all factor into a dog's susceptibility to this problem, and so does bacteria. The breed's inquisitive nature does little to help with this, as Bulldogs are known for sticking their faces into all sorts of strange places.

Keeping your dog's face and wrinkles clean will help prevent blemishes from occurring (or worsening), but to some degree the problem may not be preventable. In minor cases, all that may be necessary to clear up your dog's skin is a topical product recommended by your veterinarian. Under no circumstance should you use human acne products on your dog, as his skin is much thinner and more sensitive than our own. In severe cases, a prescription treatment, typically an antibiotic called cephalexin, may be necessary.

Brachycephalic Upper-airway Syndrome

Bulldogs are considered a brachycephalic breed—that is, they have a short, broad head and as a result frequently make loud, snorting sounds when inhaling. In and of itself, there is nothing unusual or dangerous about this. However, when certain signs are present, several serious respiratory problems may be plaguing your dog. These are often known under the umbrella term of brachycephalic upper-airway syndrome.

Symptoms

If your dog's symptoms include apparent weakness, cyanosis (bluing of the skin and mucous membranes), or fainting, have your veterinarian examine him at once. If your Bulldog is having trouble breathing, as these warning signs indicate, he needs help as soon as possible. Your vet may find that the problem besetting your dog has nothing to do with brachycephalic upper-airway syndrome, but in this situation it is always better to be safe than sorry. Since these symptoms can also indicate other afflictions, it is especially important that your dog be examined.

Your vet will listen to your Bulldog's breathing with a stethoscope and also check for any irregularities in his lungs or heartbeat. Next, he or she will check for stenotic nares, a condition in which extremely small nostril openings make breathing problematic.

Another common condition among brachycephalic breeds is an overlong soft palate, meaning that the palate reaches the base of the covering of the

Good breeding is one of the best ways to ensure a healthy dog.

larynx and the epiglottis. In severe cases, the palate can actually be sucked into the laryngeal opening when the dog inhales.

Treatment

If the problem does indeed involve your dog's breathing, there are several possible treatment options. In the mildest cases, all that may be necessary is preventing situations that exacerbate the problem. This includes limiting exercise to a reasonable amount and intensity level, as well as keeping your Bulldog cool at all times. Even if he is at rest, your dog will need air-conditioning in extremely hot and humid weather.

Another excellent precaution for dogs with this kind of breathing problem is using a harness instead of a collar. When an enthusiastic dog pulls while being walked on a conventional collar and leash, his trachea can unintentionally be compressed and further obstruct his airway.

Even minor breathing difficulties can progress into more-acute problems over time, so watch your dog to see if the problem worsens as he ages. Although surgery on a young Bulldog can be extremely successful, a surgical approach may not be an ideal option for an older pet. This makes timing an essential element to success.

Eye Problems

The easiest way to avoid one of the most common type of eye problems—injuries—is to make a concerted effort to shield your dog's eyes from common dangers both inside and outside your home. From protruding plants and bushes to sharp corners on your furniture, all sorts of things in your dog's environment can poke or scrape his eyes. Often wounds like this can result in a problem called a corneal ulcer. When an ulcer forms, it is both painful and itchy, often causing your dog to rub the area and worsen the problem. Corneal ulcers may also form as a result of bacteria or fungal infection.

Most common in young and active dogs, eye ulcers are graded according to their depth, which can vary. Prevention is ideal. If you take your dog for walks in the woods, for instance, keep the leash short, so you can help him avoid any protruding sticks or other hazards lurking in his path. When this is not possible, treatments may range from antibiotic ointments for superficial ulcers to various forms of surgical repair for more complicated situations.

Bulldogs are prone to eye injuries, so keep him away from objects like this stick.

Cherry Eye

Another common problem among Bulldogs is prolapsed gland of the third eyelid. This condition, nicknamed *cherry eye* for the unsightly red mass protruding from the corner of the dog's eye, can be quite alarming for an inexperienced or squeamish owner. Fortunately, it looks much worse than it feels, but irritation and infection can occur if cherry eye is left untreated. Like ulcerations, this condition can be caused by an injury or may appear without any physical trauma whatsoever. Frequently surgery is necessary, but in minor cases steroids are sufficient for reducing swelling.

Hip Dysplasia

A common problem in Bulldogs, hip dysplasia occurs when the hip joint is not properly formed. This may result

from a genetic predisposition or from environmental factors. Since the average age of onset is two years (the problem is nearly impossible to diagnose in dogs younger than six months old), it is extremely important that owners ask potential breeders for documentation that a puppy's parents and grandparents have been screened for hip dysplasia. Responsible breeders should be using only dogs that have received official clearance from the Orthopedic Foundation for Animals (OFA). Because the condition is not always genetic, however, even the most careful selection of a dog cannot guarantee that your Bulldog will not develop hip dysplasia.

The best way to help your dog avoid hip dysplasia is by providing him with a sensible fitness plan. Overweight dogs are particularly prone to dysplasia, so

Feeling Good

General Precautions for Anesthesia

The use of anesthesia always poses at least some risk to a pet. This is why it is imperative that medical procedures requiring your dog to be "put out" be kept to an absolute minimum. Running blood tests prior to surgery is also an excellent precaution, as this can help identify any conditions that would make the use of anesthesia inadvisable. One of the best ways to make sure your dog remains as healthy as possible is by keeping him at a healthy weight all the time, since you never know when he may need to have an unexpected operation. Overweight dogs face significantly higher risks from anesthesia.

overfeeding can increase your dog's risk. While exercise should be part of virtually any dog's routine, over-exercising can also expose your Bulldog to this problem (especially in younger dogs), so make sure your dog isn't overdoing it either. Injuries can also increase the incidence of hip dysplasia.

Symptoms

The most common symptom of hip dysplasia is pain or discomfort, especially first thing in the morning or directly following exercise. If you notice your dog limping or avoiding activity, it may be time to have him checked. By seeking treatment early, you will likely be able to relieve your pet's pain, return him to greater mobility, and prevent the unnecessary loss of muscle tone.

Treatment

Once an x-ray confirms the diagnosis, a treatment plan must be chosen. In more serious cases, surgery may be necessary. Sometimes, though, owners can improve their dog's prognosis by making smaller changes. If your dog is too heavy, reducing weight is a great place to start. Additionally, exercise that focuses on range of motion and muscle building can be extremely helpful, providing it limits stress on your dog's joints. Providing your Bulldog with warm, comfortable sleeping quarters, utilizing massage and physical therapy, and taking simple steps to make your dog's everyday activities less painful can also be beneficial.

General Illnesses

In addition to breed-specific problems, there are also some general conditions dogs can be susceptible to.

Cancer

Fortunately, cancer is no longer the automatic death sentence it once was. People and animals are beating cancer at unprecedented rates. The biggest reason is early detection. Finding a problem before it has the opportunity to become a bigger problem is hands-down the best way to fight this horrible disease. Unfortunately, just because more dogs are winning their battles with cancer, this doesn't mean that fewer animals are being diagnosed.

Making it a habit to check your dog regularly for any suspicious lumps or bumps is an excellent way to head off any potential threats to his health. If you find a lump, take your Bulldog to his vet, who will likely perform a fine-needle aspirate biopsy, depending on the location and appearance of the growth. Most tumors will end up being benign (harmless). My dog Jonathan had several so-called fatty tumors that never bothered him a bit. One, however, turned out to be malignant (cancerous). Because I discovered it early, though, my veterinarian was able to surgically remove it with impressive success.

Epilepsy

This is a condition that most often looks

much worse than it really is, so it is important to do your best to remain calm even though it may be a very scary moment for you. This, in turn, will help make it quicker and easier for your dog to return to his normal self.

A seizing dog will often shake, drool, or lose control of his bladder or bowels—or experience all these symptoms simultaneously. At first, your dog may appear dizzy and slightly disoriented. If your dog seizes, protect both him and yourself from unnecessary harm. A dog in the throes of convulsions might not even recognize his owner and may consequently bite. If the episode lasts for more than a few minutes (most vets cite the five-minute mark as the limit), or if your dog loses consciousness at any time, bring him to the nearest

Feeling Good

Contact your vet if you see changes in your Bulldog's behavior.

Senior Health Exams

Scheduling regular veterinary examinations is one of the most important steps pet owners can take to keep their pets in tip-top shape. When dogs enter the senior years, these health examinations are more important than ever. Senior care, which starts with the regular veterinary exam, is needed to catch and delay the onset or progress of disease and for the early detection of problems such as organ failure and osteoarthritis. AAHA recommends that healthy senior dogs visit the veterinarian every six months for a complete exam and laboratory testing. Keep in mind that every year for a dog is equivalent to 5 to 7 human years. To stay current with your senior pet's health care, twice-a-year exams are a must.

During the senior health exam, your veterinarian will ask you a series of questions regarding any changes in your pet's activity and behavior. The veterinarian will also conduct a complete examination of all your pet's body systems. Client education and laboratory testing are key components of the senior exam.

Aging Isn't Just Physical

With the senior years comes a general slowing down in pets. As their major senses (sight, hearing, taste, touch, and smell) dull, you may find that your dog has a slower response to general external stimuli. This loss of sensory perception often is a slow, progressive process, and it may even escape your notice. The best remedy for gradual sensory reduction is to keep your pet active —playing and training are excellent ways to keep their senses sharp.

Pets may also be affected mentally as they age. Just as aging humans begin to forget things and are more susceptible to mental conditions, your aging animals may also begin to confront age-related cognitive and behavioral changes. Most of these changes are rather subtle and can be addressed in a proactive manner. Regular senior health exams can help catch and treat these problems before they control your dog's life.

(Courtesy of the AAHA and Healthypet.com)

veterinary hospital immediately. In many cases, medication will not be necessary, but these are the circumstances that should make suppressing the problem with an anticonvulsant a practical option. Since a drug like this causes numerous side effects, though, it is preferable to avoid this route if feasible.

Dogs whose seizures begin between the ages of one and three usually suffer from idiopathic epilepsy—that is, the exact cause is unknown. In dogs over the age of four, though, seizures are far more likely to be secondary to another more serious condition if the dog has had no episodes up until this point. If you suspect your Bulldog has experienced a seizure, schedule an appointment with his veterinarian to help rule out another problem.

Keeping Track

It is highly unlikely that your vet will ever witness one of your dog's seizures, since a typical episode lasts from mere seconds to several minutes at the most. For this reason, it may be helpful to keep a log. Along with the date, time, and duration of each episode, record a detailed description of exactly what transpires, how your dog was acting before the seizure, and how long it takes him to resume normal activity afterward. Eventually, you may be able to identify certain instances when your dog is more susceptible to seizures—or even specific conditions that may trigger episodes. While you may or may not discover that your dog's seizures are prompted by a particular situation like this one, there are certain times when most dogs are more vulnerable to this problem. It is thought that most canine seizures happen between the hours of 10:00 PM and 2:00 AM, usually after a dog has spent some time sleeping. Interestingly, more seizures occur during a full moon and around the times of the solstice (i.e., the first day of winter or the first day of summer). Try to be extra vigilant during those times.

Avoiding Epileptic Triggers

My vet's dog is epileptic and tends to suffer a seizure whenever his owner goes away on a business trip. He has discovered an excellent way of interrupting this pattern. Before my vet even takes his suitcase out, he now sends his dog home with his veterinary technician for a *mini-vacation*. The dog, who adores the tech, gets to enjoy a pleasant day or two away from home with one of his favorite people—and has remarkably never had a seizure while in her care.

hormone is usually used. Although periodic blood samples should be taken to ensure proper treatment, the condition is usually highly manageable.

Alternative Therapies

Alternative medicine includes a group of traditional treatments such as acupuncture, homeopathy, and several lesser-known modalities like qi gong (pronounced chee KUNG) and the use of flower essences. Even modern physical therapy and chiropractic care employ techniques whose roots lie in these age-old practices. At one time, seeking alternative treatments was something done when all other options had been exhausted in the most desperate situations. Today, however, alternative medicine is used more and more alongside conventional techniques in treating a full range of health problems. The stigma is dissipating as Westerners are realizing the efficacy of these treatments.

Acupuncture

Acupuncture, a procedure involving the insertion of needles into specific body parts (not always the ones where the problem exists), probably raises

Hypothyroidism

A sudden weight gain can often signal a medical problem. If your dog's food intake or lack of exercise is clearly the cause, a diet and exercise plan may be all that's needed to reverse the situation. If, however, you notice an increase in weight for no apparent reason, you should ask your veterinarian if hypothyroidism could be the explanation.

In addition to weight gain, dry skin and hair loss are also signs of this endocrine disorder. When the thyroid gland is underactive, your dog's metabolism decreases, making it easier for him to gain weight. The typical age of onset is between 4 and 10 years. Once a diagnosis has been made, treatment with a synthetic thyroid more eyebrows than any other alternative treatment, but it can be surprisingly effective. Acupuncture can, for example, be used to treat torn ligaments and avoid a costly surgery. Other conditions for which acupuncture may be useful include cardiovascular disorders, chronic respiratory conditions, and gastrointestinal problems.

Homeopathy

Homeopathy involves treating a disease with infinitesimal doses of drugs that in massive amounts actually cause the disease symptoms your dog is battling. While this may sound counterproductive, it is important to note that this is the premise on which modern vaccines are based. By introducing only a minute amount of the offending agent, your dog's body is able to create an immunity against it that will subsequently react to the real threat. Even if you know a great deal about homeopathy, though, this is one treatment that should never be dabbled in or treated lightly. Because precise dosing is a must—and smaller doses can be even more powerful than larger ones with this modality—it is vital that only a trained professional be allowed to treat your dog with homeopathy.

Flower Essences

One form of alternative medicine that can be easily administered at home (with a certain amount of prior knowledge, of course) is the use of flower essences. Developed in the 1930s by Dr. Edward Bach, the practice of using these innocuous ingredients to strengthen your dog's immunity poses virtually no risk to your pet but can help him avoid numerous health problems. The underlying philosophy of this method, which involves infusing flowers and other plants in spring water, is that creating emotional balance can help fight illness and foster healing. If you think flower essences may be useful to your pet, ask your vet to recommend a particular essence or book on the topic. Since flower essences are typically administered just a drop or two at a time, remember to pick up a plastic eyedropper for your Bulldog, as a glass instrument may break and injure your pet.

To find a licensed canine acupuncturist or homeopathic caregiver in your area, contact the American Academy of Veterinary Acupuncture (AAVA) at www.aava.org or the Academy of Veterinary Homeopathy (AVH) at www.theavh.org.

Chapter 6

Being Good

Whether your Bulldog is currently enrolled in puppy kindergarten or your adult dog has never set foot in a single obedience class, the time for training is now. There are various methods of training, of course. Perhaps you enjoy the camaraderie of a class, or maybe you prefer to train in the privacy of your own backyard. Similarly, you may wish to teach your dog only a few basic commands, or you might plan to compete in formal obedience trials at some point in the future. Whatever your objective, the most important step in your dog's training will be consistency.

You needn't commit to several lengthy training sessions each day, however. In fact, spending just a few minutes daily training your pet is preferable to spending a larger block of time on the task less frequently. Training can also be fun for both you and your dog. Reward him for his achievements, and watch for signs that he's ready to call it quits for the day. By doing so, you will help ensure that he will be willing to happily return to the task tomorrow.

Socialization

Whether you realize it or not, you are always training your pets. Like children, our dogs are always looking to us to define their boundaries. If we allow them to do whatever they want, they mistakenly (but understandably) perceive that it is acceptable for them to assume the alpha role in the family. Likewise, if we show them the right way from the start, these beta, or *better*, habits instead become ingrained.

Few areas of training will have a greater impact on your Bulldog than your effort to socialize him as early and as often as possible. Fortunately, it is one of the easiest things you will ever do for your pet. Unlike housetraining or teaching your dog commands, socializing a dog requires virtually no prior knowledge of the task. It's as simple as bringing your Bulldog with you whenever and wherever you can.

How to Socialize Your Bulldog

When you take your dog for a walk, stop and chat with any friends and neighbors (or friendly strangers) you encounter on your way. Even if you just have to run a quick errand, take your dog whenever possible, and when people ask if they can pet him, say yes! Always tote along some treats for these people to offer to your Bulldog, as this will help him form a positive connotation of people.

Can you speak dog? This Bulldog's "play bow" means he's ready to have fun!

Children, too, should be encouraged to offer attention to your dog. Certainly, not all kids treat pets properly. Some mean well but simply don't understand the importance of being gentle. If you find yourself in the company of such a child, remove both yourself and your dog from the situation at once. There are plenty of opportunities for positive exchanges, but a negative interaction could leave your dog with the mistaken notion that all children behave this way. Likewise, you must make sure your Bulldog doesn't *bulldoze* any kids he encounters. An excited puppy can do just as much damage as an overly zealous child.

Can you imagine life without other people? Interacting with other canines is as important to your Bulldog as spending time with your own friends is to you. Care should always be taken when the other dog is bigger or smaller than your own, of course, but don't assume that because the dachshund across the street is tiny that he won't assert himself. Smaller dogs can often have the biggest attitudes.

Of course, you must protect your Bulldog and those who encounter him from unnecessary illness and injury. For example, until your puppy has received all his immunizations, it is wise to avoid

The Expert Knows

Do You Speak Bulldog?

"If only they could talk . . ." Many dog owners have said this. Our dogs can talk to us. They talk to us much like the people in our lives through their looks, their body language, and at times even with their silence. They may not use words like our human friends and family members, but they nevertheless speak to us—sometimes quite literally whenever they bark, growl, or fuss. Commonly, animals express themselves through their behavior, too. If a communication problem exists, it is seldom due to a lack of effort on the part of our pets but rather our own inability or unwillingness to "listen" to them. By spending time with your Bulldog and getting to know his unique ways of expressing himself, you will be surprised just how well you begin to understand what he's telling you.

places that large numbers of dogs frequent—such as dog parks, pet supply stores, etc. It is also especially important that your Bulldog is never left alone with a small child or a fellow animal. Bulldogs by nature are extremely gentle, but any dog can act out when treated improperly.

Crate Training
Crate training can be an excellent means of protecting your pet from harm when you cannot watch him, but it can also be a wonderful way to

provide your Bulldog with a place all his own. Although there are still those who believe that crating is cruel, it's a fact that most dogs long for a denlike environment away from all the commotion in their households—and a crate truly is an ideal option for these animals.

In my own home, there is something almost sacred about the crate. When my husband and I were planning the arrival of our second dog, Damon, we purchased and situated his crate well in advance. We thought this was a practical step in preparing our other dog, Molly, for the new puppy's homecoming. We fully expected her to investigate it thoroughly as soon as we set it up beside her own kennel. While she certainly did her share of sniffing it over, she never once entered his domain. Damon has now been part of our family for over a year, and he

likewise respects Molly's space the same way. They share food, toys, you name it . . . but never a crate.

How to Crate-Train Your Bulldog

The first rule when it comes to crating is to never use the kennel as punishment. If you want your dog to see his crate as a place of refuge, you mustn't turn it into a prison. Limit the amount of time your dog spends inside with the door closed—preferably no more than four hours at a time. In the beginning, you shouldn't even close the door; just give your dog a chance to spend some time inside the enclosure. If he doesn't go in on his own, tempt him with a toy or a treat, but again, leave the door open for the time being. Praise him lavishly for any time he spends there.

Once your dog seems comfortable being inside his crate, try shutting the door for short periods of time—just a minute or two at first. Again, praise him for complying. If he fusses, you must strike a balance. Open the door, but try to wait until he quiets down. Your biggest goal should be to end on a positive note. Over time, you will be able to lengthen the amount of time you leave the door closed, eventually even leaving the room for gradually increasing periods.

If your dog displays an obvious distaste for the crate, or if you yourself ultimately decide it's not for you, there is no rule that states you must use it. The crate is not a panacea; it is a tool. For some owners, it is the solution to countless problems. To some others, though, it just doesn't feel like the right choice. Remember, only you can decide what is best for you and your Bulldog.

Dogs coming from puppy mills often harbor a deep aversion to crating. After spending an unreasonable amount of time held up in such structures (and in many cases being forced to urinate and defecate within them), the crate is the last place these dogs feel safe. Trying to force these dogs to accept the crate is indeed cruel. For a dog with such a history, a safety gate is unquestionably the better option.

Housetraining

Housetraining is, without a doubt, the most dreaded task of pet ownership. You may be surprised to know, however, that when approached with consistency and a positive attitude, it can be one of the easiest accomplished training tasks. The biggest mistake many new owners make is assuming that an eight-week-old puppy is too young to begin the housetraining process. Nothing could be further from the truth! If anything, a younger dog is at an advantage, since

Bringing Up Puppy

Who can fathom the mind of a puppy? Squirrels drive them crazy, garbage is their favorite snack, and immediately after chewing your one-of-a-kind, handmade leather jacket into confetti, they can give you a look of such innocent love and adoration that you forget all about it. This kind of behavior can baffle and frustrate even the most conscientious of dog owners, and rightfully so. When you bring a puppy home, he becomes part of your family; you need to be able to trust him with your home, your belongings, and even your children. That's why controlling your puppy's behavior is the key to having a peaceful relationship with him.

To have a dog that makes a good, dependable companion, you're going to have to spend some time training. There's no other way for your puppy to know that chewing on an old knotted sweat sock is acceptable, for example, while chewing on the Irish lace tablecloth is not. He needs to be taught appropriate behavior calmly, gently, and—most important—consistently. As soon as you get your pup, you can start teaching him how to obey you, how to act around people and other dogs, and generally to be the best-behaved dog ever.

(Courtesy of the AAHA and Healthypet.com)

he hasn't had time to form poor housetraining habits. Although you may be tempted to wait a few days to allow that cute little puppy to acclimate to his new surroundings before making him begin a training routine, don't. This will make the process only more difficult for both of you.

The Importance of a Schedule

Your best housetraining tool is one you already have at home—a clock. By keeping your Bulldog puppy on a schedule, you will help ensure his housetraining success and lessen your own frustration along the way. For that eight-week-old puppy, this means heading out to his potty spot every two hours. Although this can make for a hectic routine in the beginning, the one thing you can count on is that time will fly. Before you know it, that little puppy will be three months old and ready to wait an extra hour between trips outdoors. In fact, with each additional month of age, your dog should be able to wait another hour between relieving himself. This should hit a maximum of approximately four to six hours as your dog reaches adulthood.

Feeding your dog on a schedule is just as important as taking him to relieve himself routinely. By keeping track of when your puppy eats and

drinks, you can best predict the times he will need to be taken outdoors. So discourage others from offering your puppy food between meals—at least until he has mastered the housetraining milestone. Another important part of your puppy's routine, although much harder to schedule, are his naps and playtimes. He will inevitably need to urinate after awaking from a snooze or enjoying an intense period of exercise.

Keeping Track

When I was housetraining my own dogs, I kept a chart that detailed every morsel of food they consumed, every successful trip outdoors, and every unfortunate mishap. This helped me track their progress and also identify the weakest parts of my plan. For instance, my dog Damon excelled at housetraining from the start with one

Praise your Bulldog when he eliminates in the proper place.

glaring exception. He would inevitably have an accident first thing in the morning every day. Could this have been because his tiny bladder simply couldn't handle the almost eight hours between goodnight and good morning? That likely played a part, but interestingly, the accidents lessened substantially when I realized I wasn't removing Damon's water bowl two hours before bed, as I had with our older dog, Molly, when she was housetraining. A simple epiphany but one I wouldn't have made as quickly without the help of a computer printout held by a couple of refrigerator magnets and laden with red checkmarks.

Don't punish your puppy for housetraining mistakes.

Keys to Success

Praise your Bulldog whenever he eliminates in the proper place; this is the golden ticket to future success. Although you may have seen other dog owners scold their pets for housetraining accidents, I urge you to abstain from this old-fashioned and ineffective practice. Instead ignore your dog's mistakes. Yes, ignore them. Not only will your dog not understand why you are upset (even just minutes after the deed has been done), but you may also damage your relationship with an overreaction.

Prevention

Another excellent way to set your dog up for success is preventing an accident before it happens. Most dogs display some type of pre-elimination habit. Perhaps your Bulldog paces back and forth or circles immediately before voiding his bladder or bowels, or maybe he sniffs the ground. So if you catch your dog indoors in the midst of his chosen behavior, interrupt the pattern! Make a noise to divert his attention while you grab his leash and head on out the door.

Crating

When you can't watch your dog, place him into his crate. Always provide him with a chance to eliminate both before and afterward, and avoid leaving him in there too long, with or without a break. The crate is also an ideal spot for your dog to hang out while you clean up the accidents that happen, and they will happen. If you opt not to use a crate, make sure you ask someone else in the household to escort your pup out of the room while the cleaning is done; otherwise, your dog may think it's his job to make the messes and yours to clean them up. While this may technically be true, he doesn't have to know this.

Accidents Happen

Finally, clean up thoroughly after all accidents. Dogs are extremely more likely to eliminate where they can smell traces of a previous accident. Even after you may not sense a hint of an offending odor, your dog's nose will pick up on even the smallest scent left behind. First, absorb all the wetness. Then, clean the area completely with an odor-eliminating cleaner. Several products of this kind are available at most pet supply stores; some are even available in the form of convenient wipes. Avoid products that use ammonia, though, as this is an ingredient of urine and therefore an agent likely to prompt a repeat offense.

Finding a Trainer

Dog trainers seem to be everywhere these days, and there are nearly as many different training methods as there are trainers. This is why it is imperative that you identify your goals

Bulldogs

What's the Best Age for Training?

Although puppyhood is the best time to train and socialize dogs, older dogs can learn new tricks, too. In fact, dogs of all ages can benefit from training. Dogs between 8 and 16 weeks of age should be enrolled in puppy classes. Regular classes are appropriate for dogs six months or older.

After you have selected a training program:

- Have your dog examined by your veterinarian to ensure your pet is healthy, free from parasites, and up-to-date on vaccinations.
- Don't feed your dog a large meal before class, because many trainers rely on food treats to encourage or reward desired behavior.
- Bring the training equipment recommended by the trainer.
- Practice between classes with brief lessons that end on a positive note.

By enrolling and actively participating in a dog training class, you will help your dog become not just a well-behaved member of your family but also a safer member of your community. *(Courtesy of the HSUS)*

before selecting a particular person. For example, if you know from the beginning that you want your Bulldog to participate in competitive obedience, you will want a trainer with experience in the ring. When attending events as a spectator, ask other owners which trainers they would (or wouldn't) recommend. Even if you never plan to enter a single event, the trainer you select should share your general training philosophy. For instance, do you believe in using edible rewards? The answer is less important than the fact that the two of you agree on this and other basic issues.

Ideally, you should like the person you choose, but it is even more important that he or she has a good rapport with your dog. Although you may instantly hit it off with a particular trainer, if that person isn't right for your dog, the results will be limited at best. Most important, if you get a bad feeling, keep looking. Other excellent resources for referrals are your local humane society and your dog's veterinarian. You can also contact the Association of Pet Dog Trainers (APDT) at 800-PET-DOGS (800-738-3647) or www.apdt.com for the name of a trainer in your area.

Effective Training

The most effective way to train a dog is through positive reinforcement. This can mean praising your pet vocally, providing him with edible rewards, or both. Dogs thrive when they know they have pleased their owners, so if you go with just one of these rewards, make it the praise. Nothing is a better motivator for your pet.

How Long?

Since consistency matters much more than the length of each session, make training a regular but short part of every day. In the beginning, limit the time you spend teaching a particular command to around five minutes. As your dog acclimates to the training process, gradually increase this period by five minutes at a time—with an ultimate goal of 15-minute sessions. If your dog seems open to spending

Use food rewards to train your Bulldog.

The Trick to Treating

While rewards should always play a key role in training, they should never detract from the learning experience. Edible rewards that are too crunchy or chewy, for example, may distract your Bulldog from the task at hand. Similarly, treats that are overly large can interrupt the training process with the extra time necessary to eat them. Bite-size versions of healthy foods are ideal. Cubed chicken or cheese, for example, may be a tasty departure from your dog's usual kibble, but when offered in moderation, it won't add to your dog's weight, and either one will take only seconds for him to gobble up. Be sure to lessen the amount of food your dog eats at mealtimes, though, to offset the extra calories he's consuming during training. Also, never underestimate the power of verbal praise —the most easily swallowed reward of all.

Bulldgos

more time on a particular command or task, increase the number of sessions each day as opposed to the duration of these periods. Training your Bulldog should be a fun process for both you and your dog, so always be watchful of signs that your dog is losing his focus. If he seems distracted or tired, it may be time to call it a day.

Expense
While training a dog demands a serious commitment on behalf of the owner, it does not require a great deal of expense. Most basic training classes are surprisingly economical. You may even

find that your Bulldog can learn virtually any command at home once you have learned the proper training techniques. There are countless books and videos available to assist you with this task. Basic dog training also requires little in the way of equipment. A simple leash and a pocketful of bite-size treats will take you both far. One of the most effective tools of the trade—a clicker— can be found at most pet stores and is inexpensive.

Though not a necessity, this simple plastic noisemaker works by conditioning your dog and is one of the best ways to reinforce his training success.

Basic Commands
Here are the basic commands for a well-behaved Bulldog.

Sit
The sit command is a good one to teach first, because it is truly a hands-on experience for owners and tends to be an easily mastered task for most dogs. Simply hold a treat up over your dog's nose and slowly move it back

over his head as you issue the command, "Sit." Most dogs will naturally move into the sitting position when this is done. You may then give him the treat, but don't forget to utter an enthusiastic "Good boy." Though edible rewards can be extremely effective for training, they cannot replace the power of praise.

Come

The come command is an important one. Maybe you don't think your Bulldog needs to learn a full array of obedience commands, and you're right, if that's what you think is best for you and your dog. Teaching this one word, however, can literally save your dog's life. If your Bulldog ever gets away from you, having successfully taught this single command is like having an invisible leash at your disposal.

The best way to teach this command is by catching your dog already in the act of coming to you. Whenever you see your Bulldog moving your way, say the word come in an upbeat tone, and praise him lavishly for doing so. Soon he will begin to associate the word with the

action. You can work with your dog in any safe environment—a fenced backyard or a large, open family room, for example. You can also practice with your dog on an extendable leash nearly anywhere. If working off lead, just be sure to have a friend help you, as it is especially important that you have a way of making your dog comply with the command. Most important, never admonish your dog for coming when called—if he has done something unpleasant, for instance. Your dog should never fear coming to you.

Stay

The stay command is best taught once your dog has mastered sitting. After issuing the sit command, raise your hand and say the word stay as you back up slowly. In the beginning, your Bulldog may remain still for only a few seconds, but it is especially important

Walking your Bulldog should be fun, not a struggle!

FAMILY-FRIENDLY TIP

Student Teachers

Involving the entire family in your Bulldog's training is a great way to make sure that the commands he learns stay fresh in his mind. Never assume that when a lesson is learned it is automatically ingrained. You won't have to practice a command as often, once your dog has mastered it, but you should revisit the task every now and then. A younger child may not be able to take an active role in the initial training phase but may be able to reinforce commands already taught by an adult or older child.

Just because a child is too young for participating in every aspect of training, however, doesn't mean he or she cannot be included from the beginning. If you attend a training class, ask if you may bring along fellow family members. Since space is sometimes limited, there may be a maximum number of people allowed, but even bringing your son or daughter to just one training session can help make training a family affair.

to offer praise during this time, however short.

Gradually increase the number of steps you take away from your dog.

You should also increase the amount of time before you offer praise or a reward. Eventually, your dog should be able to stay for about a minute or longer with you at least 10 feet away.

Down

Teaching the down command is most easily accomplished by using an edible reward. With your dog in a sitting position, issue the command while lowering the treat in front of him. Most dogs will naturally lower their bodies to get the treat, but if your dog does not, try slowly pulling the treat away from him. You can also draw your dog downward.

Eventually, you should start issuing the command before even bringing out the reward, as you do not want your dog's compliance to be dependent on the physical motion of lowering the treat.

Heel

If your Bulldog doesn't learn proper leash etiquette while he is young, as a strapping adult he may easily pull you off your feet and even injure himself in the process if he is allowed to pull incessantly on his walks. Teaching the heel command can help with this.

This is another command for which the sit command is a prerequisite. Begin by walking your dog on your left side with the leash in your right hand and a treat in your left. When you stop, say the word sit.

When he complies, reward him and say the word heel. Then begin walking again, stopping periodically to practice this two-part exercise. Your ultimate goal is for your dog to comfortably walk alongside you, stopping whenever you do. The heel command will be particularly useful if you plan to involve your Bulldog in formal obedience trials.

Tricks

Once you learn the basics of dog training, this valuable skill can be applied for fun as well as function. Does your Bulldog know any tricks? If not, teach him some! Whether you prefer the old standards such a shaking hands and begging or a newer favorite such as waving, the same reward-based techniques you used to teach your dog to sit and stay can be applied for these less important but equally rewarding tricks, as well.

If you're not a fan of

Using positive reinforcement, you can teach your Bulldog many tricks.

SENIOR DOG TIP

Training the Older Dog

If your older Bulldog is in need of training, be patient—with yourself and with him. It may take a senior canine a little longer to master a particular training task, but don't give up on him. Training, like so many other types of knowledge, builds on itself. As you and your dog move further into training mode, you may be surprised by how well old dogs can learn new tricks!

parlor tricks, consider teaching your dog something more practical, such as how to pick up his toys or to tell you when he needs to relieve himself. You may even consider allowing your Bulldog to take the lead in showing you which tricks he may have a knack for performing. If your dog enjoys playing games, teach him to help you look for lost items, such as your car keys or the television remote. Always reward him for a job well done, but you just may find that your dog enjoys the training process as much as the reward. There is no better reason for teaching a trick than making your dog happy.

Chapter 7

In the

Doghouse

When a problem behavior exists, it is usually the owner who needs to change something he or she is doing in order to improve the situation. Does this mean that the owner is the problem? Certainly not. It just means that it is nearly impossible to change your dog's behavior without first adjusting your own.

Many times, solving a behavior problem is a straightforward task. Occasionally, the answer is so simple, in fact, that an owner can overlook it altogether. Of course, the best way to solve any behavior problem is by preventing it. By preparing yourself for the most common issues you and your dog may face, though, you can help ensure that any issue that may arise doesn't turn into a larger problem. The first step to solving any behavior problem is ruling out a physical cause. If your dog is suffering from a medical condition, his behavior may be an important red flag. By bringing him to your vet to discuss the situation, you will be able to make sure he is healthy before approaching the problem from a behavioral standpoint.

Barking (Excessive)

Excessive barking can be frustrating for dog owners and those who live within earshot of them. The problem can quickly spiral into arguments with landlords and citations from the police. If you think your dog's barking is a problem, it is likely that others do, as well. Fortunately, this too is a situation that can be improved. When your dog barks, he is frequently trying to tell you something,

usually that he sees or hears someone or something. This is not an inherently negative behavior, as many owners appreciate being alerted to any suspicious happenings near their homes. The problem arises when the barking doesn't stop once you have been made aware of whatever has captured your dog's attention. This is why you should teach your dog the enough command.

Teaching the Enough Command

When your dog begins to bark, wait for a lapse in the noise and say the word enough as you reward him for stopping his barking at this time. You must act quickly; the lull may last for only a few seconds, making it even more important that you also choose the correct time to reward the behavior. If

Many "problem behaviors" are natural dog behaviors.

you reward too soon or too late, you will inadvertently reinforce the barking instead of the silence. Many owners find that using a clicker helps with this task immensely. This isn't always easy, but over time it is the best way to stop your dog's excessive barking without negating his more worthwhile watchdog tendencies. A good friend of mine has even taught her dogs to stop barking when she raises her index finger in front of her lips and softly says, "Shhhh."

Give your puppy appropriate items to chew on.

Chewing

Few experiences are as exasperating as discovering a treasured belonging in tattered pieces. Still, many owners of teething puppies accept this unfortunate occurrence as part and parcel of raising a dog. When the behavior continues well into adulthood, however, it becomes harder to be understanding. What's more, it can also be more difficult to correct at this age, which is why it is so important to deal with the issue from the beginning. No matter what your dog's age, he can be taught what is and isn't acceptable for chewing.

One of the biggest mistakes an owner of a chewer can do is allow him to keep an object that he has already ruined. Of course, you needn't hold on to an item your Bulldog has chewed beyond its usefulness, but by relinquishing it to him, you show him only that he inherits whatever he destroys. Remember, a reward is reinforcement!

Reinforce Appropriate Chewing

Whenever you find your dog in the midst of feasting on any item that he shouldn't be, tell him "No!" and take it away from him immediately. As simple as this may sound, it is the most important step in discouraging your dog from taking things that don't belong to him. Always offer a replacement item that *is* appropriate for him to chew, and praise him lavishly for accepting it. Never admonish him for not taking it, but continue to offer other items he may find more appealing. Also, refrain from punishing him for anything he has

In the Doghouse

already chewed. When trying to correct any problem behavior, the goal should be moving beyond the problem, not focusing on it.

Prevention

You can increase your dog's chances of success by keeping any tempting items picked up and put away. He cannot chew your sneakers, after all, if they are left securely inside your closet. Eventually, you should be able to kick off your shoes upon entering your home without the pressing need to barricade them. But in the meantime, it is best to keep any expensive or cherished items out of harm's way for both your sakes.

If the objects your Bulldog enjoys gnawing on are too large to remove— furniture, for instance—you must approach the problem a bit differently. In this case, you should still say a firm *no* and offer a replacement, but you may need to follow up by treating the item with a bitter or otherwise foul-tasting deterrent. These innocuous sprays are available at most pet supply stores and will help prevent your dog from revisiting the scene of the crime. Clove oil is also said to possess this unpleasant quality. Never use any agent that may be dangerous to your pet, however. Be patient, as you may have to treat several areas of your home before your Bulldog

gets the idea. He will get it, though, so remain persistent.

Digging

One spring day when my mother was in the middle of gardening, she noticed her dog, Jennifer, in the throes of another activity—digging. When the opportunity presented itself, she readily sank both paws into one of my mother's oversize planters and proceeded to toss every bit of the dirt into the air through her back legs as she dug deeper and deeper into the hole she had created. My mother's reaction would be to immediately grab her camera instead of discouraging her. My mother's willingness to not only tolerate this behavior but indulge it also taught me a thing or two about letting those we love be themselves.

Of course, digging is not always a celebrated event. My mother was lucky in that Jennifer didn't choose to dig often, but might that be because she allowed her the outlet when the mood did strike her? I think so. For this reason, I recommend trying to tolerate digging to some degree when possible. This doesn't mean you have to let your Bulldog dig up your begonias to have some fun, though. If your dog's digging has become a

Correcting a Senior's Bad Habits

Whether you have recently adopted an older pet, or have given up trying to correct your pet's bad habits, it is not too late to teach him good manners. From housebreaking to digging and chewing, the American Animal Hospital Association (AAHA) offers tips on how to train your problem pooch.

"Consistency and positive reinforcement are the key to training a pet of any age," says Link Welborn, DVM, AAHA past president. "In fact, older pets may be easier to train than puppies because they have a longer attention span."

- Housebreaking should be a breeze for older pets who have less urgency problems and better control. Keep a close eye on your dog or confine him to a specific area while indoors, then take him out to the same place every time to do his business. Use consistent encouragement and give him plenty of praise afterward.

- Food treats and positive reinforcement will help your pet learn basic commands such as sit, stay, and come. Plan your commands ahead of time and make sure that everyone in your household uses the same commands so your pet doesn't get confused.

- Toys aren't just for puppies. Older pets also need stimulating toys and plenty of exercise to prevent them from digging and chewing out of boredom. Keeping a close watch over your pet so he doesn't have an opportunity to misbehave, and using consistent praise to reinforce good behavior, should eliminate most behavior problems.

- The key to any training regimen is consistent, positive reinforcement of the desired behavior rather than punishment. Never physically punish a pet; this may lead to biting out of fear, or other aggressive behavior. Instead, use praise and attention as a reward when the desired behavior is exhibited and ignore inappropriate behavior.

- If your pet continues to display unwanted behaviors despite your best efforts, visit your veterinarian to discuss the problem. The veterinarian will examine your pet to rule out anything medical that could be causing or contributing to the behavior, as well as provide advice and additional resources to help solve the problem. Your veterinarian can also refer you to a behavior specialist.

(Courtesy of the AAHA and Healthypet.com)

problem, consider why he may be doing it. Perhaps he is heading to your begonias because, like these flowers, he is seeking out some shade, a cool spot to rest on a hot day. Instinctually, many dogs dig for just this reason. Or maybe he is trying to escape the confines of your yard. This may be the problem if your dog digs when a neighboring dog is in heat or being walked past your fence regularly.

Diversions

Diversion is usually the most effective tool when it comes to dealing with digging. When your dog starts digging, offer a firm "No!" Once you have interrupted the activity, present him with a favorite toy or treat to entertain him instead. Praise him for accepting it. You may find, however, that he then wants to bury the special item for later. If this is the case, I strongly recommend reserving a special spot of the yard

where he can do just that. Whenever his digging ventures beyond the borders of this space, again, interrupt the action and redirect him to his own spot. If you absolutely don't wish to deal with digging, make every effort to nip it in the bud whenever you witness the activity. Provide distractions, praise compliance, and try to limit the time your dog spends outdoors alone. A proficient digger should never be trusted to stay in the yard alone, as just one escape could be deadly.

Housesoiling

One of the most common behavior problems is housesoiling, or inappropriate elimination. Housesoiling is often the result of incomplete housetraining, but it can also indicate a medical problem. For this reason, it is vital that you have your dog checked by his veterinarian before approaching the situation through behavior modification.

If there is no physical cause, some changes must be made. Whether your two-year-old Bulldog seems to have regressed in his elimination habits, or you adopted a dog who was simply never reliably housetrained in the first place, the problem can be solved, but both patience and persistence will be necessary.

Excitable Wetting

The approach your dog needs will depend somewhat on the timing of his accidents. For example, if your dog predictably loses control of his bladder when you walk through the door each day, the problem is likely excitable wetting. To avoid this problem, you must ignore your dog completely whenever entering your home after an absence. As someone who has dealt with this issue personally, I can tell you that the length of time you have been away has absolutely no bearing on the need for this step. My own dogs greet me with the same enthusiasm whether I have been gone all day or have run a 15-minute errand. If I pet them immediately upon walking through the door, the flood gates are instantly opened. I have also noticed that using a high-pitched voice when greeting them can also elicit this same reaction.

Submissive Urination

Another common scenario is submissive urination. This is when a dog wets himself whenever confronted by a fellow animal or person whom he sees as his superior. Frequently, the dog acts in other submissive ways, as well—such as rolling onto his back. The solution here is similar to that of excitable wetting. Avoid giving your dog direct attention whenever you enter the room. He may still submit to you when you do approach him, but the most common time for submissive urination is when first coming into contact with the superior party. Also, try getting down to his level by kneeling instead of bending over him (a universally dominant form of body language) when you are ready to greet your dog.

If the superior individual is another animal, socialization can help. Just like people, dogs have different personalities. If yours tends to be on the shy side, getting him out to meet other dogs can help boost his confidence and bring him out of his

Always ID

A pet—even an indoor pet—has a better chance of being returned if he always wears a collar and an ID tag with your name, address, and telephone number. Ask your local animal shelter or veterinarian if permanent methods of identification (such as microchips) are available in your area.

shell a bit. Again, he may still allow other animals to hold a higher position in the hierarchy, but you can lessen the intensity of his reactions through frequent exposure.

Marking

Finally, there is one other reason your dog may be eliminating inappropriately: marking. If your dog is urinating as a means of identifying his territory, sterilization may help. Intact dogs—both male and female—are more likely to stake their claim in this way.

If accidents seem to be happening for no reason at all, remedial training must begin. Start by praising your dog whenever he eliminates in the proper spot. Positive reinforcement goes a long way in any kind of dog training, but punishment will likely only hurt your chances of improving the situation. Another vital measure is instituting (or re-establishing) a schedule for your pet. This should include the times he is given opportunities to eat, exercise, and eliminate. Sometimes solving a housesoiling problem is as easy as refraining from offering treats outside this routine. Another common problem is not allowing a dog a sufficient number of trips outdoors each day. If you notice that most accidents are happening at a particular time of day, you may simply need to take your Bulldog outside during this

period so he doesn't use your furniture as a comfort station.

Jumping Up

Most Bulldogs love people, so receiving company is usually one of their favorite pastimes. While there is nothing wrong with your dog giving your friends an enthusiastic greeting whenever they arrive at your home, jumping up on visitors can quickly become an unpleasant habit if tolerated. You may not mind it when your dog jumps on you—and perhaps even many of your friends don't either, but at some point

Encouraging your Bulldog to jump up can lead to bad habits.

your 50-pound (23 kg) dog will likely encounter someone who understandably *does* mind. Moreover, as well intended as he may be, your dog could hurt someone, particularly a child. Even if you rarely entertain friends in your home, the possibility of your dog encountering someone in your home or on the street who is afraid of dogs is a real possibility. This is why it is particularly important that you never indulge this behavior.

Teaching No Jumping

Teaching a dog not to jump up can actually be a lot of fun for both you and your pet. The best way to train him to remember his manners when greeting guests is by practicing. Ask a friend or relative whom your dog is especially fond of to help you with this task. When he or she repeatedly *arrives* at your door, your dog will have the opportunity to practice his welcoming ritual many times in a single day. Allow him to offer kisses while happily wagging his tail, and encourage your friend to offer him attention in response to his actions, but if at any time he jumps up, immediately tell him "No!" and then instruct him to sit. Occasionally, a dog is so excited by seeing one of his favorite humans that the *down* command may be necessary.

Your friend must also make a point of ignoring your Bulldog as soon as he jumps. Continuing to provide him with attention will only reinforce the

FAMILY-FRIENDLY TIP

Safety First

Teaching kids how to properly treat animals is just as important as training your Bulldog how to behave well around children. If your dog is struggling with a problem behavior, it is even more vital that your son or daughter act appropriately when in the presence of your pet. Your primary responsibility is to set limitations that keep both your kids and your Bulldog safe. If your child is older, he or she may be able to help in your dog's extended training. If not, limit his or her involvement to offering praise once you and your pet have rounded the corner toward some success. If your dog's problem is aggression, you mustn't allow him any interaction with your child until you are confident the situation has been permanently resolved.

behavior. When your dog complies with your commands, your friend may return to greeting him—as long as he refrains from further jumping. After a short break, ask your friend to go back outside and re-enter your home to practice this scenario again. You may repeat the exercise as many times as your Bulldog continues to show excitement over your friend's entrance.

Eventually, you probably won't even have to tell your dog to sit; he will do so all on his own. Your future guests will think he is merely showing off his good manners, but you will know his secret—that he is actually just ensuring that he gets what he wants most, attention.

Nipping

While other problem behaviors may be bothersome, a biting dog can be downright dangerous. If your Bulldog is showing signs of aggression, action must be taken right away to correct the problem. If tolerated, even an occasional tendency to nip can quickly spin out of control.

Signs of aggression can vary from a barely audible growl when someone moves toward your dog's food bowl to a more threatening baring of the teeth for what appears to be no reason at all. Although playful biting may seem innocent, even this early inclination to use his teeth can signal the beginning of a legitimate problem for your dog. As cute or harmless as it might seem, dissuade your Bulldog puppy from chewing on your hands during play. Allowing him

to place his mouth on your body is the first step in teaching him that biting is acceptable, a lesson no dog should ever learn.

When a dog acts aggressively primarily around food or toys, the owner must remove the problem item at the first sign of the issue. It is especially important that you do not get into a power struggle with your pet, so refrain from punishing him. But you must uphold your role as the alpha member of the family. When you reintroduce the item—be it food or anything else, remain involved in the process. Gently place your hand in your dog's dish, or even better, feed him by hand. If it is a toy that you have returned to him, take it back occasionally. If he growls, again take it away. Repeat this process as many times as necessary.

If you find yourself feeling fearful of your dog or you just can't seem to improve the situation on your own, it is wise to enlist the help of a professional. Begin by talking to your dog's veterinarian. He or she will likely be able to recommend a dog trainer or animal behaviorist in your area. What matters most is that you seek the help you need.

If you find your Bulldog is too possessive about his toys, contact a trainer or behaviorist for help.

Should I Contact a Behaviorist?

Not every dog who growls needs intense training, and not every case of howling indicates an underlying problem like separation anxiety. So how do you know when your Bulldog needs the additional help of a dog trainer or animal behaviorist? If you have tried to solve the problem repeatedly on your own but can't seem to find a workable solution, it may be time to turn to a professional. Likewise, it may be time to seek help if your dog is acting aggressively. This most serious behavior problem must always be dealt with in a timely manner.

Ignoring the problem will only allow it to become worse—and place you, your dog, and anyone he encounters in harm's way.

Finding a Behaviorist

Unlike a trainer whose work focuses primarily on teaching your dog obedience-related commands, an animal behaviorist observes, interprets, and modifies animal behavior—most often once a serious problem has already arisen. A trainer may be able to help you correct mild behavior problems, but for more intense problems, a behaviorist is often the best person for the job.

Behaviorists are commonly called into the picture when an animal suffers from a phobia, aggression, or another serious behavioral disorder. Sometimes a dog and his owner struggle with more than one of these problems, making the advice of this professional even more valuable. But where can you find such a person?

Like trainers, animal behaviorists do not currently need to be licensed in order to work in this specialized field, so careful selection is a must. Although a certification process exists, there are currently only a limited number of certified individuals. You can find a directory at www.animalbehavior.org. You can also ask your veterinarian, trainer, or local Bulldog rescue organization to recommend a behaviorist.

Above all else, you should feel comfortable with the person you choose, but there a few other important issues that should factor into your decision. Your behaviorist should possess a certain level of education and experience in dealing with animals, particularly dogs. He or she should also have dog training knowledge and experience. A degree of some form in psychology or zoology is a definite advantage. Ask for references, and be sure to follow up on them. References from former clients are good, but recommendations from veterinarians and humane societies are even better.

Chapter 8

Stepping Out

Your Bulldog will want to tag along with you wherever you go. Whether the destination is more about him—visiting the park or the pet supply store, or the focus is more mundane—picking up the dry cleaning or stopping by the post office, your Bulldog will never cease to delight in keeping you company.

Travel and Vacationing

For some Bulldog owners, a vacation simply isn't a vacation without the whole family there to join in on the fun. Many dogs also enjoy being included in their owners' travel plans, but precautions need to be taken to ensure their safety during any trip.

By Air

For Bulldogs, the most important thing to remember is that flying in a plane's cargo compartment is dangerous. While other breeds may be able to tolerate the extreme temperatures of this area, a Bulldog's tendency toward breathing difficulties makes the risk you take by placing him in this part of the plane a potentially deadly one. If your Bulldog puppy is still small enough to ride in a carrier in front of your seat, your airline may allow him to ride in the cabin with you, but if not, it is best to skip flying altogether.

By Car

Care must also be taken when hitting the road with your Bulldog, but this alternate form of transportation offers the flexibility of creating your own itinerary—and adjusting it accordingly whenever the need arises. Take frequent breaks along the way to wherever you are going, and be sure to keep your vehicle well ventilated. Most important, make sure your dog has a safe and secure place to ride (his crate is ideal), and never leave him alone in a

Bulldogs

SENIOR DOG TIP

Going Along for the Ride

You may think you are doing your older Bulldog a favor by allowing him to rest quietly at home while you travel, but unless you will be flying (or your dog has a medical condition that makes travel inadvisable), he will likely be a lot happier by your side.

Still, it is always best to plan ahead in hopes of avoiding any small problems that may arise. First, make sure your Bulldog is comfortable. Schedule your trip for a time when the weather is neither too hot nor too cold. Pad your dog's crate with an orthopedic foam liner. This will give him the best of both worlds—the ability to join you on vacation and the luxury of that quiet rest all the while. Next, make sure your dog stays properly hydrated. Bring along fresh water and take frequent breaks for drinks. Finally, don't forget your dog's first-aid kit. The contents? Anything your veterinarian recommends adding to it. You can ask him or her about this when you have your Bulldog examined and cleared for travel shortly before your trip, perhaps the most important precaution you should take before traveling with your senior pet.

parked car. Canine seat belts are offered by many pet supply retailers, but these are often more practical for those trips to the dry cleaner than for longer road trips. In his crate, your dog can move around a bit and relax as you make your way to your destination. You might think the only time a closed car is a danger is when the weather is hot, but interior temperatures can also soar in the middle of winter when a car's heater is left running. Leave the windows open, though, and you run the unacceptable risk of your dog's theft. If you must enter an establishment where your Bulldog is not welcome, ask one of your traveling companions to stay behind with him for the short time you will be gone.

Quick stops like these are an excellent time to provide your Bulldog with a drink and an opportunity to relieve himself. Feed your dog only a light meal prior to the trip, and avoid feeding him again until you will be stationary for at least a few hours. This will help prevent motion sickness along the way. Cracking a window and positioning your dog's crate so he can see outside the vehicle are also smart preventive measures. Although your dog can't tell you with words that he is feeling nauseous, he will likely show some

warning signs when he is feeling queasy, such as yawning or drooling. If your dog often experiences intense symptoms (such as vomiting), ask your veterinarian about giving him motion sickness medication prior to your trip.

What to Bring

Whether you are leaving for a day trip or an extended vacation, your best resource is a well-planned checklist of everything you'll need. Since space is often limited, though, you must focus on items of true necessity. So how do you decide if an item is worthy of a spot in your Bulldog's suitcase? Ask yourself two basic questions: Is this something he uses every day, and would he need it in the event of an emergency? If either answer is yes, it should go with you.

Your Bulldog will love riding in the car with you, but use a crate to keep him safe.

The Travel Bag Equation: Double the Function Equals Half the Headaches

Items that serve dual purposes are especially helpful when traveling. Not only do these convenient must-haves keep your bags from overflowing, but they also make caring for your pet while on the road an easier task. A thermos, for example, can function as both a way to transport fresh water for your Bulldog and a bowl from which he can drink it. Your dog's crate will help keep him safe while riding and also offer him a comfortable and familiar bed once you reach your destination. My favorite multipurpose items are by far the most economical, though. Zip-style plastic bags can help organize your pet's belongings, serve as impromptu water bowls, and work wonderfully for various kinds of cleanups, and baby wipes can help with everything from spills to cleaning your dog's wrinkles. The most important item you should bring along can also serve a dual purpose. When assembled with a little planning, a first-aid kit will come in handy for either you or your dog in the event of a medical emergency. Some of the most useful items—antibiotic ointment, rubbing alcohol, and hydrogen peroxide just to name a few—can be used both on people and on animals.

Sports and Activities

Dogs—even those of the same breed—can have amazingly different personalities. Because of this, they often enjoy spending their time in very different ways. If your dog is in particularly good physical shape and has lots of energy, agility might be his thing. Perhaps your Bulldog has a more docile nature; if so, obedience training may be for him. Expose your pet to different activities, and watch for signs that you have found the right match for his individual strengths.

Agility

The *non-sporting* breed. That says it all, doesn't it? Although the Bulldog isn't your typical

If you are staying at a pet-friendly hotel with a pool, keep an eye on your Bulldog— remember he can't swim.

canine athlete, he enjoys being active just as much as the next dog. In fact, this breed's playful nature makes him an ideal match for a pastime such as agility, an activity that combines the fun of exercise with the challenge of dexterity. Resembling an equestrian jumping competition, the setting for agility consists of a variety of colorful jumps, vaulted walks, seesaws, A-frames, and tunnels. Handlers lead their dogs through the course by running alongside them and offering either verbal commands or hand signals (or both) as the dogs navigate these obstacles.

Agility can be as fun for spectators as it is for participants, and the sport regularly draws impressive crowds. Developed in England in the 1970s, it was first recognized by the AKC in 1994. Unlike the requirements for conformation, a dog need not be purebred to compete in agility, and entrants may also be spayed or neutered. The one requirement that is more stringent, however, is a minimum of age of 12 months for all canine participants.

Titles that can be earned in agility are: Novice Agility Dog (NAD), Open Agility Dog (OAD), Agility Dog Excellent (ADX), and Master Agility Excellent (MAX). Not everyone who participates pursues all these levels, however, or competes in every competition. The best thing about agility is that it is something you can

Sports and Safety

Whether you are attending a conformation event or simply playing with your Bulldog in your own backyard, one of the most common causes for concern is the heat. Even with emergency treatment, heatstroke can be fatal. The best cure is prevention, and your dog is relying on you to keep him out of harm's way. Summer does not have to be fraught with peril—with ample precaution, both you and your pet can enjoy those long, hot dog-days of summer. Signs of heatstroke: Panting; Staring; Anxious expression; Refusal to obey commands; Warm, dry skin; High fever; Rapid heartbeat; Vomiting; Collapse

(Courtesy of the AAHA and Healthypet.com)

do with your Bulldog right in your own backyard. You need not ever enter a formal competition to participate, though it might be a whole lot of fun!

Obedience

If your Bulldog shows an affinity for obedience training, you may consider involving him in formal obedience competition. Like agility, obedience is a pastime that welcomes both pedigreed and mixed-breed dogs. Unlike the sport of agility, though, which focuses on a dog's physical abilities and allows considerable owner interaction, obedience requires more discipline than athleticism. It is truly a test of how well your dog can do on his own. Among the commands your Bulldog will be required to perform at the basic level of competitive obedience are heeling (both on and off lead), sitting and staying for several minutes at a

time, and also standing and staying for similarly fixed time periods. Training for obedience is no small task; owners must spend a considerable amount of time with their pets during this process. As soon as the competition begins, though, they must step back and let their dogs demonstrate what they have learned. Owners are allowed to issue commands, of course, but they must refrain from coaxing or cheering until their dogs

The activity levels of Bulldogs can vary widely; find an activity best suited to your individual Bulldog.

are finished with their individual exercises.

Dogs begin competing in the Companion Dog (CD) class and then move on to the Companion Dog Excellent (CDX) class, and Utility Dog (UD) class. Ultimately, your Bulldog has the potential of earning the highest titles—Obedience Trial Champion (OTCh) and Utility Dog Excellent (UDX). Both are considered prestigious accomplishments that are neither easily nor quickly achieved.

Showing (Conformation)

Every owner is proud of his or her dog, but Bulldog owners seem to revel just a bit more than the average person in celebrating their dog's unique appeal. They deeply enjoy spending time with their pet, they delight in talking about him, and they absolutely bask in showing him off. For some, this means chatting with neighbors while taking their dog for walks, but for others the audience is a bit broader, and the events are considerably more formal.

Conformation events (more commonly called dog shows) began as a means of evaluating breeding stock, but over time they have evolved into a source of great entertainment and education for participants and onlookers. Bulldogs may be entered in multibreed shows as members of the non-sporting group or in specialty events that feature only a single breed. Points (ranging from one to five) are issued for each win, and dogs who accumulate a total of 15 points or more earn the right to use the title Champion (or Ch.) before their name.

Games

Perhaps you discovered your dog's affinity for agility while playing together more informally in your backyard, or maybe you first noticed his aptitude for obedience while teaching him to gently take a cookie from your mouth. Yes, hobbies are often borne of less structured but equally fun pastimes like these. Sometimes, though, playtime is just that—play. This does not mean that leisure time is wasted time. On the contrary, there is often great value in thinking outside the ring, so to speak. By making time for impromptu and creative play, you encourage your dog to show you where his interests and talents truly lie. And you will both undoubtedly have a great time in the process.

Whatever games you choose (or invent), the most important thing is that you make time for play as often as possible. With the busy nature of our day-to-day lives becoming more and more hectic, the recreation will do both you and your dog a world of good. At no other time will your Bulldog ever be so relaxed, so carefree, or more himself.

FAMILY-FRIENDLY TIP

The Waiting Game

There's a reason that doctors fill their waiting rooms with magazines: No one enjoys waiting. Kids and pets are no different in this way. Pediatricians often offer an excellent variety of both children's books and toys to entertain the kids while they wait, making routine appointments go much more smoothly. If you have a child, you have likely employed this same strategy when heading out on a road trip with your son or daughter. Why not use it for your Bulldog, as well? Just like your kids, your dog will tire of the road quickly if he has nothing to hold his attention. Always bring along a few of your dog's favorite things to comfort him and stimulate him during a trip. Avoid noisy toys, as these will do little for your own sense of relaxation. Chew toys are ideal, as they allow your pet to entertain himself. Be sure to pack a few different choices, though, so you can rotate them during a lengthy ride. Consider placing these alternate items in a plastic bag inside a cooler. Nothing will refresh your weary canine traveler on a hot day more than an ice-cold toy.

Resources

ASSOCIATIONS AND ORGANIZATIONS

Breed Clubs

American Kennel Club (AKC)
5580 Centerview Drive
Raleigh, NC 27606
Telephone: (919) 233-9767
Fax: (919) 233-3627
E-mail: info@akc.org
www.akc.org

Canadian Kennel Club (CKC)
89 Skyway Avenue, Suite 100
Etobicoke, Ontario M9W 6R4
Telephone: (416) 675-5511
Fax: (416) 675-6506
E-mail: information@ckc.ca

Federation Cynologique Internationale (FCI)
Secretariat General de la FCI
Place Albert 1er, 13
B – 6530 Thuin
Belqique

The Kennel Club
1 Clarges Street
London
W1J 8AB
Telephone: 0870 606 6750
Fax: 0207 518 1058
www.the-kennel-club.org.uk

United Kennel Club (UKC)
100 E. Kilgore Road
Kalamazoo, MI 49002-5584
Telephone: (269) 343-9020
Fax: (269) 343-7037
E-mail: pbickell@ukcdogs.com

Pet Sitters

National Association of Professional Pet Sitters
15000 Commerce Parkway,
Suite C
Mt. Laurel, New Jersey 08054
Telephone: (856) 439-0324
Fax: (856) 439-0525
E-mail: napps@ahint.com

Pet Sitters International
201 East King Street
King, NC 27021-9161
Telephone: (336) 983-9222
Fax: (336) 983-5266
E-mail: info@petsit.com

Rescue Organizations and Animal Welfare Groups

American Humane Association (AHA)
63 Inverness Drive East
Englewood, CO 80112
Telephone: (303) 792-9900
Fax: 792-5333
www.americanhumane.org

American Society for the Prevention of Cruelty to Animals (ASPCA)
424 E. 92nd Street
New York, NY 10128-6804
Telephone: (212) 876-7700
www.aspca.org

Royal Society for the Prevention of Cruelty to Animals (RSPCA)
Telephone: 0870 3335 999
Fax: 0870 7530 284
www.rspca.org.uk

The Humane Society of the United States (HSUS)
2100 L Street, NW
Washington DC 20037
Telephone: (202) 452-1100
www.hsus.org

Sports

International Agility Link (IAL)
Global Administrator: Steve Drinkwater
E-mail: yunde@powerup.au
www.agilityclick.com/~ial

North American Dog Agility Council
11522 South Hwy 3
Cataldo, ID 83810
United States Dog Agility Association
P.O. Box 850955
Richardson, TX 75085-0955
Telephone: (972) 487-2200

Therapy

Delta Society
875 124th Ave NE, Suite 101
Bellevue, WA 98005
Telephone: (425) 226-7357
Fax: (425) 235-1076
E-mail: info@deltasociety.org

Therapy Dogs Incorporated
PO Box 5868
Cheyenne, WY 82003
Telephone: (877) 843-7364
E-mail: therdog@sisna.com
www.therapydogs.com

Therapy Dogs International (TDI)
88 Bartley Road
Flanders, NJ 07836
Telephone: (973) 252-9800
Fax: (973) 252-7171
E-mail:
www.tdi-dog.org

Training

Association of Pet Dog Trainers (APDT)
150 Executive Center Drive
Box 35
Greenville, SC 29615
Telephone: (800) PET-DOGS
Fax: (864) 331-0767
E-mail: information@apdt.com
www.apdt.com

National Association of Dog Obedience Instructors
PMB 369
729 Grapevine Hwy.
Hurst, TX 76054-2085

Veterinary and Health Resources

Academy of Veterinary Homeopathy (AVH)
P.O. Box 9280
Wilmington, DE 19809
Telephone: (866) 652-1590
Fax: (866) 652-1590
E-mail: office@TheAVH.org
www.theavh.org

American Academy of Veterinary Acupuncture (AAVA)
100 Roscommon Drive, Suite 320
Middletown, CT 06457
Telephone: (860) 635-6300
Fax: (860) 635-6400
E-mail: office@aava.org
www.aava.org

American Animal Hospital Association (AAHA)
P.O. Box 150899
Denver, CO 80215-0899
Telephone: (303) 986-2800
Fax: (303) 986-1700
E-mail: info@aahanet.org
www.aahanet.org/index.cfm

American College of Veterinary Internal Medicine (ACVIM)
1997 Wadsworth Blvd., Suite A
Lakewood, CO 80214-5293
Telephone: (800) 245-9081
Fax: (303) 231-0880
Email:

American College of Veterinary Ophthalmologists (ACVO)
P.O. Box 1311
Meridian, Idaho 83860
Telephone: (208) 466-7624
Fax: (208) 466-7693
E-mail: office@acvo.com

American Holistic Veterinary Medical Association (AHVMA)
2218 Old Emmorton Road
Bel Air, MD 21015
Telephone: (410) 569-0795
Fax: (410) 569-2346
E-mail: office@ahvma.org
www.ahvma.org

American Veterinary Medical Association (AVMA)
1931 North Meacham Road – Suite 100
Schaumburg, IL 60173
Telephone: (847) 925-8070
Fax: (847) 925-1329
E-mail: avmainfo@avma.org
www.avma.org

ASPCA Animal Poison Control Center
1717 South Philo Road, Suite 36
Urbana, IL 61802
Telephone: (888) 426-4435

British Veterinary Association (BVA)
7 Mansfield Street
London
W1G 9NQ
Telephone: 020 7636 6541
Fax: 020 7436 2970
E-mail: bvahq@bva.co.uk
www.bva.co.uk

Canine Eye Registration Foundation (CERF)
VMDB/CERF
1248 Lynn Hall
625 Harrison St.
Purdue University
West Lafayette, IN 47907-2026
Telephone: (765) 494-8179
E-mail: CERF@vmbd.org

Orthopedic Foundation for Animals (OFA)
2300 NE Nifong Blvd
Columbus, Missouri 65201-3856
Telephone: (573) 442-0418
Fax: (573) 875-5073
Email:

Publications

Magazines

AKC Family Dog
American Kennel Club
260 Madison Avenue
New York, NY 10016
Telephone: (800) 490-5675
E-mail: familydog@akc.org
www.akc.org/pubs/familydog

AKC Gazette
American Kennel Club
260 Madison Avenue
New York, NY 10016
Telephone: (800) 533-7323
E-mail: gazette@akc.org
www.akc.org/pubs/gazette

Dog & Kennel
Pet Publishing, Inc.
7-L Dundas Circle
Greensboro, NC 27407
Telephone: (336) 292-4272
Fax: (336) 292-4272
E-mail: info@petpublishing.com
www.dogandkennel.com

Dog Fancy
Subscription Department
P.O. Box 53264
Boulder, CO 80322-3264
Telephone: (800) 365-4421
E-mail: barkback@dogfancy.com
www.dogfancy.com

Resources

Index

Note: **Boldface** numbers indicate illustrations.

111

Index

Dedication

To my mother Norma and my father Daniel, who truly believe I can do anything. I love you both. And as a parent myself now, I finally understand just how much you love me.

Acknowledgments

I would like to thank the following people for taking the time to speak with me about their experiences with Bulldogs: Lacey Brushwood, Lone Star Bulldog Club and Rescue; Connie Cochran, Breeder; Frank "Sonny" Seiler, Owner of University of Georgia mascot, Uga; Lesa Strickland, Lone Star Bulldog Club and Rescue, Bulldog Club of America. Special thanks go to Nancy Rose, DVM, for answering every one of my endless questions and sharing her special insight as both a veterinarian and a breeder with me.

About the Author

Tammy Gagne is a freelance writer who specializes in the health and behavior of companion animals. She is a regular contributor to several national pet care magazines and has owned purebred dogs for more than 25 years. In addition to being an avid dog lover, she is also an experienced aviculturist. She resides in northern New England with her husband, son, dogs, and parrots.

Photo Credits

REACH OUT. ACT. RESPOND.

Go to AnimalPlanet.com/ROAR and find out how you can be a voice for animals everywhere!